ID0844301

DATE DUE

GAYLORD			PRINTED IN U.S.A.

Eating Disorders

Arthur Gillard, *Book Editor*

GREENHAVEN PRESS
A part of Gale, Cengage Learning

GALE
CENGAGE Learning™

Detroit • New York • San Francisco • New Haven, Conn • Waterville, Maine • London

Christine Nasso, *Publisher*
Elizabeth Des Chenes, *Managing Editor*

© 2010 Greenhaven Press, a part of Gale, Cengage Learning

Gale and Greenhaven Press are registered trademarks used herein under license.

For more information, contact:
Greenhaven Press
27500 Drake Rd.
Farmington Hills, MI 48331-3535
Or you can visit our Internet site at gale.cengage.com

For product information and technology assistance, contact us at

Gale Customer Support, 1-800-877-4253
For permission to use material from this text or product, submit all requests online at www.cengage.com/permissions

Further permissions questions can be e-mailed to permissionrequest@cengage.com

Articles in Greenhaven Press anthologies are often edited for length to meet page require-ments. In addition, original titles of these works are changed to clearly present the main thesis and to explicitly indicate the author's opinion. Every effort is made to ensure that Greenhaven Press accurately reflects the original intent of the authors. Every effort has been made to trace the owners of copyrighted material.

Cover image copyright © Bubbles Photolibrary/Alamy

LIBRARY OF CONGRESS CATALOGING-IN-PUBLICATION DATA

Eating disorders / Arthur Gillard, book editor.
    p. cm. -- (Issues that concern you)
  Includes bibliographical references and index.
  ISBN 978-0-7377-4952-6 (hardcover)
 1. Eating disorders. I. Gillard, Arthur.
  RC552.E18E2821118 2010
  616.85'26--dc22   2010004547

Printed in the United States of America
1 2 3 4 5 6 7 14 13 12 11 10

CONTENTS

Eating disorders are widely considered to be a modern phenomenon. Anorexia nervosa was clinically defined in 1873, bulimia was classified as a disorder in 1903, and binge-eating disorder was not officially recognized until 1992. Although clinicians knew about eating disorders as far back as the nineteenth century, it was not until the 1970s that the general public started to become aware of the problem, particularly with the publication of psychiatrist Hilde Bruch's book *The Golden Cage: The Enigma of Anorexia*. Through the 1980s and 1990s and into the twenty-first century, much more information on the subject has become available in the form of books, movies, Web sites, and other resources.

Yet descriptions of conditions we would now recognize as eating disorders can be found far back in history. In "Historical Understandings," an article on MentalHelp.net, psychologist Bridget Engel et al. note:

> Historical evidence suggests that anorexia and bulimia have existed since at least the first century. During the time of Caesar (700 B.C.), rich ancient Romans overindulged at lavish banquets and then relieved themselves by vomiting so they could return to the feast and continue eating. Ancient Egyptians drew hieroglyphics that depicted their use of monthly purges to avoid illness. Persian medical manuscripts, and Chinese scrolls originating in early dynasties also describe ailments that are very similar to modern eating disorders. The vast body of tribal lore from Africa contains several stories concerning adults who fasted during times of extreme famine in order to save food for their children, and then continued to restrict their diet and were in danger of dying even after the famine was over.

The first known case of a fatality from anorexia is that of a woman—a follower of St. Jerome—who starved herself to death in

A.D. 383. During the medieval period and the Renaissance many cases of eating disorders were described, perhaps most famously Saint Catherine, who lived from 1347 to 1389. As reported by Haley Feuerbacher in "Saintly Sickness: Catherine of Siena as a Prototype of Holy Anorexia":

> If Catherine forced herself to swallow even a mouthful, she vomited and claimed that she was unable to eat; according to Catherine, eating would kill her, so she would rather die of starvation than gluttony. . . . Catherine tried to eat once a day but only chewed bitter herbs and spit out the substance. If she did ingest any food, she would purge it immediately, claiming that her vomiting was a means of penance.

Many claim that such historical accounts are not the same as modern cases of eating disorders. Journalist Irene Lagan, in her InsideCatholic.com article "Catherine of Siena and the Origin of Eating Disorders," notes, "If St. Catherine was extreme in her penitential practices, she was motivated by love of God, not the angst and self-loathing that characterizes the pathology of eating disorders and other self destructive behavior." Others believe that cases of bingeing and purging in ancient Rome do not truly constitute bulimia, since it was a socially accepted practice at the time and occurred in public festivals.

Such controversies over the historical record may simply reflect our evolving understanding of eating disorders. At one time the cause of eating disorders was thought to be purely physical—for example, anorexia was thought to be a form of tuberculosis, a result of hormone imbalances or endocrine deficiencies. In the 1930s emotional and psychological issues began to be seriously considered by the medical community as partly involved in causing these illnesses; the case study of Ellen West, a patient of Swiss psychiatrist Ludwig Binswanger from 1930 to 1933, was one of the first to seriously consider the interior perspective of a patient suffering from an eating disorder, with his written accounts using her poetry and excerpts from her diary to illustrate her emotions and psychological state.

The first known case of anorexia was Saint Catherine of Siena, who starved herself to death in A.D. *383.*

More recently much attention has been focused on the influence of the culture and the media. For example, philosopher Chris Kraatz believes that

> the nation's eating disorders epidemic will not subside until we pull together and make deep and lasting social and cultural change. . . . The diagnosis of an eating disorder reveals at least as much about the cultural environment as it does

about the individual. That means that the focus of change necessary to facilitate healing needs to be at least as much on the cultural environment as it does on the individual.

However, eating disorders are so complex and multifaceted that probably all of these factors hold part of the truth. As Jim Kirkpatrick and Paul Caldwell write in *Eating Disorders: Everything You Need to Know:*

> In the development of an eating disorder, internal factors such as genetics, biochemical makeup and personality traits combine with external pressure from family, peers and society. Although one or more of these influences may be more prominent in one person than in another, it is usually the combination that leads to the disorder, rather than one single event or personality trait.

Authors in this anthology offer a variety of perspectives on eating disorders. In addition, the volume contains several appendixes to help the reader understand and explore the topic, including a thorough bibliography and a list of organizations to contact for further information. The appendix titled "What You Should Know About Eating Disorders" offers facts about eating disorders. The appendix "What You Should Do About Eating Disorders" offers advice for young people who have an eating disorder or know someone who does. With all these features, *Issues That Concern You: Eating Disorders* provides an excellent resource for everyone interested in this issue.

ONE

An Overview of Eating Disorders

National Institute of Mental Health

> The mission of the National Institute of Mental Health, a U.S. government institution, is to increase understanding and treatment of mental illnesses through research and education, leading to better prevention, recovery, and cures. The following viewpoint gives an overview of the three most common eating disorders, which are anorexia nervosa, bulimia nervosa, and binge-eating disorder; for each disorder, symptoms and treatment approaches are described. Because antidepressants are often prescribed to treat symptoms of eating disorders, the authors emphasize recent research showing a significantly increased risk of suicide in young people taking this kind of medication, which has resulted in very strong warnings by the Food and Drug Administration. They also briefly discuss current research approaches to help better understand eating disorders.

An eating disorder is marked by extremes. It is present when a person experiences severe disturbances in eating behavior, such as extreme reduction of food intake or extreme overeating, or feelings of extreme distress or concern about body weight or shape.

A person with an eating disorder may have started out just eating smaller or larger amounts of food than usual, but at some point, the urge to eat less or more spirals out of control. Eating

National Institute of Mental Health, "Eating Disorders," nimh.nih.gov, June 12, 2009.

disorders are very complex, and despite scientific research to understand them, the biological, behavioral and social underpinnings of these illnesses remain elusive.

The two main types of eating disorders are anorexia nervosa and bulimia nervosa. A third category is "eating disorders not otherwise specified (EDNOS)," which includes several variations of eating disorders. Most of these disorders are similar to anorexia or bulimia but with slightly different characteristics. Binge-eating disorder, which has received increasing research and media attention in recent years, is one type of EDNOS.

Eating disorders frequently appear during adolescence or young adulthood, but some reports indicate that they can develop during childhood or later in adulthood. Women and girls are much more likely than males to develop an eating disorder. Men and boys account for an estimated 5 to 15 percent of patients with anorexia or bulimia and an estimated 35 percent of those with binge-eating disorder. Eating disorders are real, treatable medical illnesses with complex underlying psychological and biological causes. They frequently coexist with other psychiatric disorders such as depression, substance abuse, or anxiety disorders. People with eating disorders also can suffer from numerous other physical health complications, such as heart conditions or kidney failure, which can lead to death.

Eating Disorders Are Treatable Diseases

Psychological and medicinal treatments are effective for many eating disorders. However, in more chronic cases, specific treatments have not yet been identified.

In these cases, treatment plans often are tailored to the patient's individual needs that may include medical care and monitoring; medications; nutritional counseling; and individual, group and/or family psychotherapy. Some patients may also need to be hospitalized to treat malnutrition or to gain weight, or for other reasons.

Anorexia Nervosa

Anorexia nervosa is characterized by emaciation, a relentless pursuit of thinness and unwillingness to maintain a normal or healthy weight, a distortion of body image and intense fear of gaining weight, a lack of menstruation among girls and women, and extremely disturbed eating behavior. Some people with anorexia lose weight by dieting and exercising excessively; others lose weight by self-induced vomiting, or misusing laxatives, diuretics or enemas.

Many people with anorexia see themselves as overweight, even when they are starved or are clearly malnourished. Eating, food and weight control become obsessions. A person with anorexia typically weighs herself or himself repeatedly, portions food carefully, and eats only very small quantities of only certain foods. Some who have anorexia recover with treatment after only one episode. Others get well but have relapses. Still others have a more chronic form of anorexia, in which their health deteriorates over many years as they battle the illness.

According to some studies, people with anorexia are up to ten times more likely to die as a result of their illness compared to those without the disorder. The most common complications that lead to death are cardiac arrest, and electrolyte and fluid imbalances. Suicide also can result.

Many people with anorexia also have coexisting psychiatric and physical illnesses, including depression, anxiety, obsessive behavior, substance abuse, cardiovascular and neurological complications, and impaired physical development.

Other symptoms may develop over time, including:

- thinning of the bones (osteopenia or osteoporosis)
- brittle hair and nails
- dry and yellowish skin
- growth of fine hair over body (e.g., lanugo)
- mild anemia, and muscle weakness and loss
- severe constipation
- low blood pressure, slowed breathing and pulse
- drop in internal body temperature, causing a person to feel cold all the time
- lethargy

Treating anorexia involves three components:

1. restoring the person to a healthy weight;
2. treating the psychological issues related to the eating disorder; and
3. reducing or eliminating behaviors or thoughts that lead to disordered eating, and preventing relapse.

Some research suggests that the use of medications, such as antidepressants, antipsychotics or mood stabilizers, may be modestly effective in treating patients with anorexia by helping to resolve mood and anxiety symptoms that often co-exist with anorexia. Recent studies, however, have suggested that antidepressants may not be effective in preventing some patients with anorexia from relapsing. In addition, no medication has shown to be effective during the critical first phase of restoring a patient to healthy weight. Overall, it is unclear if and how medications can help patients conquer anorexia, but research is ongoing.

Different forms of psychotherapy, including individual, group and family-based, can help address the psychological reasons for the illness. Some studies suggest that family-based therapies in which parents assume responsibility for feeding their afflicted adolescent are the most effective in helping a person with anorexia gain weight and improve eating habits and moods.

Shown to be effective in case studies and clinical trials, this particular approach is discussed in some guidelines and studies for treating eating disorders in younger, nonchronic patients.

Others have noted that a combined approach of medical attention and supportive psychotherapy designed specifically for anorexia patients is more effective than just psychotherapy. But the effectiveness of a treatment depends on the person involved and his or her situation. Unfortunately, no specific psychotherapy appears to be consistently effective for treating adults with anorexia. However, research into novel treatment and prevention approaches is showing some promise. One study suggests that an online intervention program may prevent some at-risk women from developing an eating disorder.

Bulimia Nervosa

Bulimia nervosa is characterized by recurrent and frequent episodes of eating unusually large amounts of food (e.g., binge-eating), and feeling a lack of control over the eating. This binge-eating is followed by a type of behavior that compensates for the binge, such as purging (e.g., vomiting, excessive use of laxatives or diuretics), fasting and/or excessive exercise.

Bulimia nervosa is characterized by episodes of binge-eating followed by purging.

Unlike anorexia, people with bulimia can fall within the normal range for their age and weight. But like people with anorexia, they often fear gaining weight, want desperately to lose weight, and are intensely unhappy with their body size and shape. Usually, bulimic behavior is done secretly, because it is often accompanied by feelings of disgust or shame. The bingeing and purging cycle usually repeats several times a week. Similar to anorexia, people with bulimia often have coexisting psychological illnesses, such as depression, anxiety and/or substance abuse problems. Many physical conditions result from the purging aspect of the illness, including electrolyte imbalances, gastrointestinal problems, and oral and tooth-related problems.

Other symptoms include:

- chronically inflamed and sore throat
- swollen glands in the neck and below the jaw
- worn tooth enamel and increasingly sensitive and decaying teeth as a result of exposure to stomach acids
- gastroesophageal reflux disorder
- intestinal distress and irritation from laxative abuse
- kidney problems from diuretic abuse
- severe dehydration from purging of fluids

As with anorexia, treatment for bulimia often involves a combination of options and depends on the needs of the individual.

To reduce or eliminate binge and purge behavior, a patient may undergo nutritional counseling and psychotherapy, especially cognitive behavioral therapy (CBT), or be prescribed medication. Some antidepressants, such as fluoxetine (Prozac), which is the only medication approved by the U.S. Food and Drug Administration for treating bulimia, may help patients who also have depression and/or anxiety. It also appears to help reduce binge-eating and purging behavior, reduces the chance of relapse, and improves eating attitudes.

CBT that has been tailored to treat bulimia also has shown to be effective in changing bingeing and purging behavior, and eating attitudes. Therapy may be individually oriented or group-based.

Common Symptoms of Eating Disorders

Symptoms	Anorexia Nervosa	Bulimia Nervosa	Binge-Eating Disorder
Excessive weight loss in relatively short period of time			
Continuation of dieting although very thin			
Dissatisfaction with appearance, belief that body is fat, even though severely underweight			
Loss of monthly menstrual periods			
Unusual interest in food and development of strange eating rituals			
Eating in secret			
Obsession with exercise			
Serious depression			
Bingeing			
Vomiting or use of drugs to stimulate vomiting, bowel movements, and urination			
Bingeing but no noticeable weight gain			
Disappearance into bathroom for long periods of time			
Abuse of drugs or alcohol			

Binge-Eating Disorder

Binge-eating disorder is characterized by recurrent binge-eating episodes during which a person feels a loss of control over his or her eating. Unlike bulimia, binge-eating episodes are not followed by purging, excessive exercise or fasting. As a result, people with binge-eating disorder often are overweight or obese. They also experience guilt, shame and/or distress about the binge-eating, which can lead to more binge-eating.

Obese people with binge-eating disorder often have coexisting psychological illnesses including anxiety, depression, and personality disorders. In addition, links between obesity and cardiovascular disease and hypertension are well documented.

Treatment options for binge-eating disorder are similar to those used to treat bulimia. Fluoxetine and other antidepressants may reduce binge-eating episodes and help alleviate depression in some patients.

Patients with binge-eating disorder also may be prescribed appetite suppressants. Psychotherapy, especially CBT, is also used to treat the underlying psychological issues associated with binge-eating, in an individual or group environment.

FDA Warnings on Antidepressants

Despite the relative safety and popularity of SSRIs and other antidepressants, some studies have suggested that they may have unintentional effects on some people, especially adolescents and young adults. In 2004, the Food and Drug Administration (FDA) conducted a thorough review of published and unpublished controlled clinical trials of antidepressants that involved nearly 4,400 children and adolescents. The review revealed that 4% of those taking antidepressants thought about or attempted suicide (although no suicides occurred), compared to 2% of those receiving placebos.

This information prompted the FDA, in 2005, to adopt a "black box" warning label on all antidepressant medications to alert the public about the potential increased risk of suicidal thinking or attempts in children and adolescents taking antidepressants. In

2007, the FDA proposed that makers of all antidepressant medications extend the warning to include young adults up through age 24. A "black box" warning is the most serious type of warning on prescription drug labeling.

The warning emphasizes that patients of all ages taking antidepressants should be closely monitored, especially during the initial weeks of treatment. Possible side effects to look for are worsening depression, suicidal thinking or behavior, or any unusual changes in behavior such as sleeplessness, agitation, or withdrawal from normal social situations. The warning adds that families and caregivers should also be told of the need for close monitoring and report any changes to the physician. The latest information from the FDA can be found on their Web site at www.fda.gov.

Results of a comprehensive review of pediatric trials conducted between 1988 and 2006 suggested that the benefits of antidepressant medications likely outweigh their risks to children and adolescents with major depression and anxiety disorders. The study was funded in part by the National Institute of Mental Health.

How Are Men and Boys Affected?

Although eating disorders primarily affect women and girls, boys and men are also vulnerable. One in four preadolescent cases of anorexia occurs in boys, and binge-eating disorder affects females and males about equally.

Like females who have eating disorders, males with the illness have a warped sense of body image and often have muscle dysmorphia, a type of disorder that is characterized by an extreme concern with becoming more muscular. Some boys with the disorder want to lose weight, while others want to gain weight or "bulk up." Boys who think they are too small are at a greater risk for using steroids or other dangerous drugs to increase muscle mass.

Boys with eating disorders exhibit the same types of emotional, physical and behavioral signs and symptoms as girls, but for a variety of reasons, boys are less likely to be diagnosed with what is often considered a stereotypically "female" disorder.

Current Research on Eating Disorders

Researchers are unsure of the underlying causes and nature of eating disorders. Unlike a neurological disorder, which generally can be pinpointed to a specific lesion on the brain, an eating disorder likely involves abnormal activity distributed across brain systems. With increased recognition that mental disorders are brain disorders, more researchers are using tools from both modern neuroscience and modern psychology to better understand eating disorders.

One approach involves the study of the human genes. With the publication of the human genome sequence in 2003, mental health researchers are studying the various combinations of genes to determine if any DNA variations are associated with the risk of developing a mental disorder. Neuroimaging, such as the use of magnetic resonance imaging (MRI), may also lead to a better understanding of eating disorders.

Neuroimaging already is used to identify abnormal brain activity in patients with schizophrenia, obsessive-compulsive disorder and depression. It may also help researchers better understand how people with eating disorders process information, regardless of whether they have recovered or are still in the throes of their illness.

Conducting behavioral or psychological research on eating disorders is even more complex and challenging. As a result, few studies of treatments for eating disorders have been conducted in the past. New studies currently underway, however, are aiming to remedy the lack of information available about treatment.

Researchers also are working to define the basic processes of the disorders, which should help identify better treatments. For example, is anorexia the result of skewed body image, self esteem problems, obsessive thoughts, compulsive behavior, or a combination of these? Can it be predicted or identified as a risk factor before drastic weight loss occurs, and therefore avoided?

These and other questions may be answered in the future as scientists and doctors think of eating disorders as medical illnesses with certain biological causes. Researchers are studying behavioral questions, along with genetic and brain systems information, to understand risk factors, identify biological markers and develop medications that can target specific pathways that control eating behavior. Finally, neuroimaging and genetic studies may also provide clues for how each person may respond to specific treatments.

TWO

Disordered Eating and Obsessive Exercise Form a Dangerous Cycle

Heather Arsenault

Heather Arsenault was an intern at the National Women's Health Network and currently works as the public policy manager at the National Association for Biomedical Research. In the following viewpoint Arsenault tells the story of how her own obsession with athletics gradually led to a serious eating disorder. She argues that personality characteristics associated with successful athletes—such as perfectionism, compulsiveness, and expectations of high achievement—put them at particular risk for developing eating disorders. Arsenault states that particular sports in which leanness is considered a competitive advantage, for example, gymnastics and swimming, are more likely to lead to eating disorders. She concludes that because of this increased risk, early prevention education is very important.

It's difficult to pinpoint exactly when my obsession with food, diet, and exercise began. From a young age, I was always smaller than my peers, and remained on the low end of the height and weight charts. I was a very active child, involved in several ath-

Heather Arsenault, "Disordered Eating and Obsessive Exercise: The Dangerous Cycle," *Women's Health Activist*, vol. 34, January/February 2009. Copyright © 2009 National Women's Health Network. Reproduced by permission.

letic activities from an early age, including swimming, soccer, gymnastics, and track and field. My parents were physically active, as well. My mom taught aerobics at the local YWCA, and both my mom and dad cycled, ran, and frequented the gym.

Origins of an Eating Disorder

The first time I remember being concerned with my weight was around the age of 10, when I began to compete as a gymnast. I was by no means overweight, and was probably underweight, but I remember feeling self-conscious around the other girls in my skin-tight leotard. Around this time, I also began to notice that most of the really good gymnasts were small and lean, with seemingly no body fat. I watched the Olympic gymnasts on television and

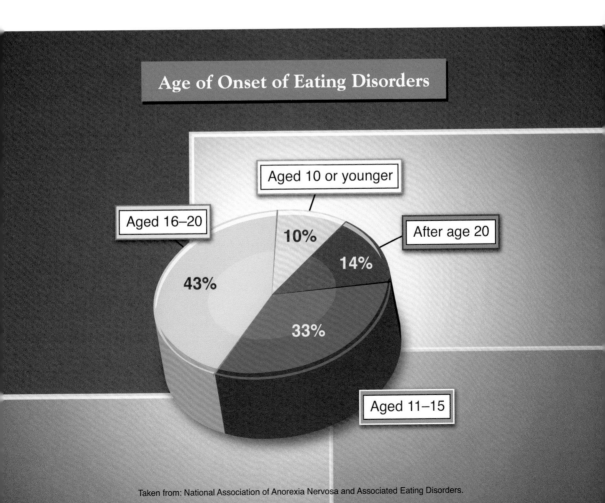

Age of Onset of Eating Disorders

Aged 10 or younger

Aged 16–20

After age 20

10%

14%

43%

33%

Aged 11–15

Taken from: National Association of Anorexia Nervosa and Associated Eating Disorders.

was impressed by their lean, strong, and agile bodies. I remember being amazed that some of these girls were in their late teens and even early twenties because they all looked much younger, or at least their bodies did. This was the first time that I associated being lean with having superior athletic ability and performance.

In junior high, I began to run cross-country. I absolutely loved both the sport and the feeling that came with running long distances. I was smaller and faster than most of my team mates, and running came easily to me. By the time I was in seventh grade, I was winning most of my cross-country meets with relative ease. I loved winning, and the confidence that gave me.

In high school, I began to notice that my body wasn't maturing as quickly as the other girls were, although it didn't bother me. I enjoyed being thin, and was pretty sure that it enabled me to run faster and win more. The more competitive I became in cross-country, the more conscious I was of the foods I ate, and how much I put into my body. I consciously cut down on my food intake and became very interested in nutrition, specifically athletic performance nutrition. Though I don't know where I got this idea from, at some point I came to believe that consuming foods that contained any amount of fat was bad. I made a conscious decision to omit fat entirely from my diet. I started to read all food labels and shied away from eating foods that didn't have a label. I was pretty much hungry all of the time, which wasn't surprising, given the amount of energy I expended in training and competing. Yet, I was terrified of gaining weight and jeopardizing my running performance. I wanted to maintain a competitive edge and that, to me, meant staying very lean. I was obsessed with fitness and nutrition. In the process, I prevented my body from maturing. As a senior in high school, I was 5'3" and 95 pounds—underweight by all standards.

The first significant break I took from running was during the winter of my senior year. I had already been accepted to a top ten, Division I college's women's cross-country team. I needed a little break to enjoy my senior year and to behave more like my peers. During the month that I took off from running, I also eased up on my strict eating habits, and allowed myself to eat some foods

Sports such as gymnastics that emphasize maintaining a lean body weight can lead to eating disorders.

that contained fat. Within four weeks, I had gained close to ten pounds. I was not happy. Everyone told me that I looked great, but I didn't like the new shape that my body had assumed. To my dismay, I looked like a young woman instead of a prepubescent teen. I was not at all comfortable in my new skin. This discomfort initiated what turned into many years of unhealthy dieting and exercise practices driven by poor body image.

Athletic Personality Traits and Eating Disorders

My story is not unlike that of many young, female athletes. Studies show that athletes are far more prone to developing eating disorders than are non-athletes. The highest prevalence of eating disorders exists among female athletes who compete in sports where leanness is considered important for performance: such as gymnastics, figure skating, swimmers, and runners. Furthermore, personality traits that are advantageous to competitive athletics (such as perfectionism, compulsiveness, and high achievement expectations) are also commonly associated with eating disorders.

A Norwegian study of elite female athletes sought to identify risk factors for eating disorders. Interestingly, the study found that training for a specific sport before the body matures can provoke a conflict in which the athlete struggles to prevent the natural physical changes brought about by growth and maturity. For me, this was clearly the cause of great inner turmoil.

The Necessity of Prevention Education

Prevention education is crucial to addressing eating disorders and exercise obsession. Athletes, parents, coaches, training staff, and doctors need to be taught the risks and warning signals of disordered eating and compulsive exercise. It's critical for them to be aware that young gymnasts, swimmers, figure skaters and long distance runners are at an elevated risk for developing an eating disorder. Special care should be taken with these young athletes to prevent stunting their growth and maturation, which, in turn, increases the likelihood of an eating disorder. Another strategy for handling this obsession is to stress to the young athlete the importance of a strong body, which is very important if the athlete intends to pursue his or her sport in the future. The potential dangers of restrictive dieting to the body should be addressed, such as the possibility of anemia, stress fractures, and other injuries. This harsh reality could serve as a deterrent to the serious athlete.

It's no wonder that I developed an unhealthy obsession with food (or an eating disorder, as I still cringe to call it). I fit the eating disordered personality profile to a "T." It took stepping back from my behaviors, and allowing myself to relax and have fun, to realize how neurotic my habits had become. It didn't take long before I realized just how much joy in everyday activities I was missing due to my obsession with both food and exercise. Luckily, I had a wonderful support system of friends and family to help me through the transition which was, at times, not easy. To this day, I occasionally struggle with diet, exercise, and body image. I'm not entirely sure that anyone could have prevented my obsession with running, and I'm not even sure that I regret it. I do wish, however, that someone had intervened with my compulsive dieting. It would have saved me years of emotional, psychological, and physical anguish.

THREE

African American Girls Struggle with Body Issues

Lola Adesioye

Lola Adesioye is a British writer and commentator who lives in New York. She specializes in issues affecting the African American community. In the following viewpoint Adesioye discusses how African American beauty standards have differed in the past from mainstream American cultural expectations, but says that this is changing as minority groups increasingly adopt Western beauty standards. She states that the rate of bulimia is actually much higher among poor and African American groups, but argues that eating disorders in such individuals are often not recognized or treated because so many people, including doctors and other treatment providers, falsely believe that only young, wealthy, white women suffer from these conditions.

For a long time it's been widely believed that eating disorders affect a certain type of woman. Open any women's magazine, read the latest story about a female celebrity and her weight and you'll know what I mean. Apparently these disorders affect mostly young, well-off white women—the Lindsay Lohans and Mary-Kate Olsens of this world.

Meanwhile, the black and Latina female stars are shown flaunting their curves and being bootylicious. They are lauded for their willingness to embrace their natural shapes, rather than starve them out of existence. The popular preconception is that women of colour don't have eating disorders. Apparently we love our hips, thighs and butts unconditionally.

There's no doubt that many of us do—but according to the latest findings [2009] from a group of economists at the University of Southern California, it's clear that it's not just white girls with serious eating problems.

Bulimia Rates Are Higher than Thought

While researching another issue related to eating disorders, the USC economists stumbled on a surprising nugget of information: bulimia—a disorder generally found to be more prevalent among black women than anorexia—is significantly more common among black girls than previously thought. In fact, "girls who are African-American are 50% more likely than girls who are white to be bulimic and girls from families in the lowest income bracket studied are 153% more likely to be bulimic than girls from the highest income bracket".

The story of eating disorders among black women is an untold, and often an unknown, one.

There are good reasons why black women have been thought to be immune from eating disorders. Many of my white girlfriends have had an eating disorder at some point in their lives. I have been involved in more than a few conversations with them in which a desire to be thinner or the admiration of some ultra-thin female celebrity has been the subject of discussion. Among my black girlfriends I can't think of one who has—or has admitted to having—had an eating disorder. Weight-related discussions with my black female friends also tend to be very different—the emphasis is never on being thin.

Beauty Standards Are Changing

Research has shown that even though there are more overweight African-American women than white women, black

Research has shown that although more African American women are overweight than white women, they rate themselves more highly in body satisfaction than do white women.

women generally rate themselves more highly in terms of body satisfaction and body confidence. Black women are also said to define beauty in broader terms: beauty is not based just on body size, but on how a woman carries herself, the clothes she wears and even factors like how her hair is done. Plus, in black culture, a curvier and more thick-set body is considered desirable and attractive. One friend of mine (she's a natural size 0) is desperately trying to put on weight because she wants to be bigger and curvier.

But this is changing—and the picture is becoming more complex as minority and mainstream cultural ideas collide. It has been suggested that the more a black woman adopts western standards of beauty—which tend to equate being thin with being beautiful—the more likely she is to suffer from an eating disorder.

I can attest to this. At the age of 15, I was curvy. At a predominantly white all-girls school, I had a hard time feeling comfortable in my body when I was surrounded by thin white friends and teen magazines which held up women who looked totally different from me as paragons of beauty.

Eating Disorders in African Americans Are Often Unrecognized

These notions of what is deemed attractive in different cultures may also be the reason why so many black girls' eating disorders go undetected and underreported. A black woman with an eating disorder may not be willing to talk about it for fear of being ridiculed for going against cultural norms.

Similarly, if researchers believe that black women are less likely to suffer from eating disorders, they are probably less likely to study them. Furthermore, doctors may be less likely to diagnose and subsequently treat an eating disorder in a black girl because he or she wouldn't be looking for one. These cultural notions may have some truth to them, but it's becoming clearer that they may be more myth than reality.

A change in the way in which eating disorders are examined, and a new approach to how and who is educated about the issue, are necessary. Previous research that has suggested that white women are more likely to suffer from eating disorders has been based on who was receiving treatment for the condition.

Given that treatment is based on a variety of factors such as socio-economic status (i.e., being able to afford treatment in the first place), and even cultural beliefs about receiving treatment by

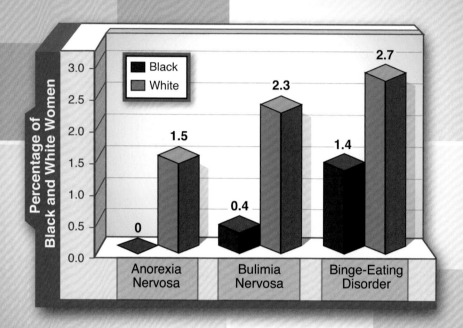

Eating Disorders Among Black and White Women

Percentage of Black and White Women

- Black
- White

	Anorexia Nervosa	Bulimia Nervosa	Binge-Eating Disorder
Black	0	0.4	1.4
White	1.5	2.3	2.7

Taken from: Maternal and Child Health Bureau, U.S. Department of Health and Human Services.

psychiatrists and psychologists, it's easy to see why black women would have escaped notice. This is particularly true when taking into account that this particular research has found that it is girls from lower income and less educated families—those less likely to seek or be able to afford treatment—who are most at risk.

Obesity is a significant issue within African-American communities, and this too has been found to come along with disordered eating, with some using purging to control the binges. Along with obesity education, more information and education about bulimia and other eating disorders need to be directed towards black girls.

Most important, anyone who deals with eating disorders—including parents, friends and educators—needs to change her assumptions. The truth is that black women have body-image issues just like any woman.

FOUR

Boys and Men Also Suffer from Eating Disorders

Anna Patterson

Anna Patterson lived for fourteen years with chronic anorexia and is the author of several books on eating disorders, including her autobiographical account *Anorexic*, a novel about eating disorders called *Running On Empty*, and *Fit to Die: Men and Eating Disorders*. In the following viewpoint Patterson discusses the factors that lead men to develop eating disorders, arguing that media and advertising adversely affect men as well as women, causing them to feel their bodies are inadequate. She says certain professions and sports, such as wrestling, swimming, and bodybuilding, are particularly associated with these disorders in men. Patterson states that low self-esteem and other psychological issues can lead some men to an unhealthy obsession with developing a lean, muscular body type. Since, according to Patterson, such disorders often go unnoticed in men, she gives some tips on identifying these problems early on so that they can be treated.

There is now a growing number of men [with eating disorders]. It is still unclear exactly how many as research into men and eating disorders is twenty years behind that of women. Unfortunately some doctors do not recognise that eating disorders

Anna Patterson, "Men with Eating Disorders," MaleHealth.co.uk, March 6, 2005. Reproduced by permission. This article first appeared on malehealth.co.uk, the health information Web site of the Men's Health Forum.

are a problem for men and as a result, a number of cases have not been correctly diagnosed.

Men may also find it hard to recognise that they have a problem. Whereas women are constantly kept informed by the media about cases of anorexia and bulimia, men rarely see evidence of the condition. Unfortunately, this means they are less likely to seek help early on in the development of their condition. On average, it seems to be approximately six years before men will seek help for their eating problems and by this time the condition will have become chronic.

When a media campaign highlights the issue of male eating problems though, the number of men seeking help increases dramatically.

How Eating Disorders Affect Men

Women seem to worry about whether they are fat or ugly but with men it is usually slightly different. They are more concerned with how they see themselves, and their self-worth is linked to how strong, in control and productive they are in their lives. They need to feel a success in all areas of their life—work, exercise, background, friends, home life etc. If a man feels inadequate in different areas of his life then it is possible that problems can develop.

Like women, men suffer from all the various kinds of eating disorders although binge eating seems to be the most prevalent problem. There are also differing concerns for both men and women. Research has shown that women are more concerned with their weight, whereas men tend to focus on their shape and muscle definition.

Men today [in 2005] are spending 58% more on fitness related activities than five years ago. A large percentage of the economy is now dependant on the current fixation with thinness for both men and women.

It has been reported that men's dissatisfaction with their body has tripled over the last thirty years. In increasing numbers, men are having plastic surgery and liposuction has become especially

Eating Disorders in Men and Women

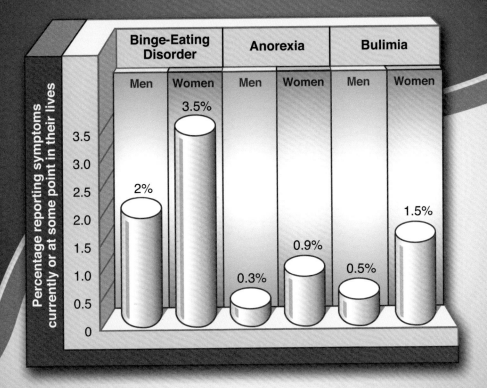

	Binge-Eating Disorder		Anorexia		Bulimia	
	Men	Women	Men	Women	Men	Women
	2%	3.5%	0.3%	0.9%	0.5%	1.5%

Percentage reporting symptoms currently or at some point in their lives

Taken from: Eve Bender, "Eating-Disorder Data Show Extensive Comorbidities," *Psychiatric News*, March 2, 2007.

popular. Between 1999 and 2000 there was a 23% increase in the number of cosmetic procedures performed on men.

It is said that women 'dress to impress' but men in contrast work out to compete with other men. There is a strong competitive element in most men that leaves them feeling inadequate around any man who has a tighter, more muscular body. Men who have smaller bodies are often considered 'weedy' and used in advertising campaigns as figures of fun—for example the 'Mr Muscle' cleaning products campaign. This can lead men to feel that unless they have a strong muscular body, they are a failure.

Why Men Get Eating Disorders

Eating disorders in men (as in women) are not about food or weight but are in fact emotional problems. They develop as a way of coping with the conflicts, stresses and pressures in life. An eat-

Low self-esteem and other psychological issues can lead some men to obsess about their weight and body image.

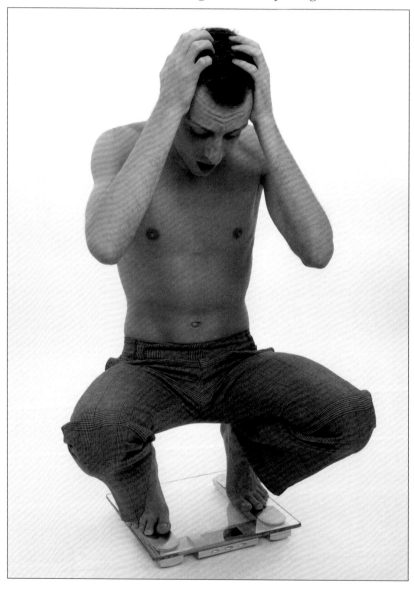

ing disorder may seem like a way of exerting control for a person who feels that their life is out of control.

People with eating disorders have been known to range from as young as eight to men in their sixties. However, the majority of men state that their problems began during their childhood years. Many remember being overweight in their teens and as a result were singled out and bullied or called names.

It does seem that whereas women are more likely to be at a normal weight when they develop an eating disorder, men are frequently overweight.

The original reasons why they were overweight as children are frequently linked to problems at home, crises at school or difficulty coming to terms with growing up. This low self-esteem coupled with the issues surrounding their weight can lead to eating disorders.

As the numbers of overweight children is increasing, it is very important that teachers and parents are aware of the effect that being overweight can have on a child and the possibility of eating disorders developing.

Like women, men are also at risk of different types of abuse during their childhood years (mental, physical and sexual). Research has shown that many men with eating disorders experienced childhood sexual abuse. This is often an experience which men feel unable to discuss due to feelings of shame. They are concerned that they will be accused of 'bringing the abuse upon themselves'. Often, victims blame themselves and feel certain that others will blame them too.

It is now widely acknowledged that eating disorders are a way of coping with the stresses of life. Traditionally, men are known to turn to drink or possibly drugs as a way of dealing with the issues in their life which they find impossible to solve. In contrast, women are seen as more frequently turning to eating disorders for their 'solution'. It now seems that these boundaries are [beginning] to blur however and as society changes and places more importance on men 'looking good', eating disorders are increasing in the male population.

Possible Indicators of Eating Disorders in Males

The onset of an eating disorder in males is usually due to a specific trigger or set of triggers. For men, these include:

- Experiences of childhood bullying/teasing due to being overweight.
- Low self-esteem because of issues during childhood (examples of which are incest, rape or mental torment).
- Parental strictness, especially from a father. This often extends to control over food and ritualised mealtimes.
- Bodybuilding and obsessive exercising.
- Specific occupations such as athletics, dance, horse racing, etc.
- History or family history of being overweight.
- Difficulties dealing with being gay.
- Having a parent with a serious weight related illness such as heart disease or diabetes.
- A fear of developing sexual feelings. (Anorexia causes a drop in male testosterone levels, which leads to a lack of sexual feelings and desires.)

Stresses frequently increase at specific points in a person's life and this can trigger a dormant eating disorder to become active. For example, a number of men have stated that when they went to college, their eating disorder became worse.

Other stressful times can be during a relationship break-up, illness of a parent, starting or changing a job and starting or changing a school or college.

For older men, triggers may include: excessive job responsibilities, divorce, marital problems, children leaving for college and the death of a parent or close family member.

Men often change their diet or exercise habits when they see a parent fall ill, especially if the illness is diet or weight related. Fear of having similar health problems such as heart disease or a stroke can cause a man to radically change his dietary habits and this has been shown as a cause of some eating disorders developing.

The Role of the Media and Advertising

Many women now feel free to objectify men's bodies in the way that theirs have been treated for so many years. This has meant that men have started to feel self-conscious about their body shape. They are constantly seeing images in magazines, on billboards and on television of the 'perfect' male body.

It seems that in the same way that women are expected to have the 'perfect' size 8 body, men are expected to have 99.9% lean muscle definition. Men now have their own 'body beautiful' magazines and *Men's Health* has become a top seller. Like women, men have now started to count calories, exercise daily and constantly compare themselves to the models on the magazine covers.

It seems that it is men in their teens, 20s and 30s who are most affected by such imagery that is now portrayed by adverts [advertisements] and other media agencies. Older men grew up in a time when the male body was hidden.

How the 'Ideal' Male Body Shape Has Changed

A [1999] study has compared the action figures of the '70s and '80s with those of today and there has been an enormous increase in the musculature.

In 1974, a GI Joe doll . . . had a 44 inch chest, 31 inch waist and 12 inch biceps. The GI Joe of today has a 50 inch chest, 28 inch waist and 22 inch biceps. It seems that an increase in musculature, especially on the upper body, is the new 'desirable' shape.

Recent male role models have been extremely muscular. Film stars such as Arnold Schwarzenegger, Sylvester Stallone, Dolph Lundgren, Vin Diesel and all the WWE [World Wrestling Entertainment] wrestling stars portray the image that large muscles and power are essential masculine traits.

This increasing trend for such muscular bodies is a concern. Some researchers do not believe that it is possible to have a figure of the proportions demonstrated by the dolls without resorting to the use of steroid supplements. Certainly there has been an increase in the number of men resorting to supplements to try and increase their size and muscular definition. Anabolic steroids are very dangerous and can cause psychotic reactions such as hallucinations, manic symptoms and depression.

The Relationship Between Exercise and Eating Disorders

Men are far more likely to turn to exercise to deal with their body shape issues than women, who usually choose dieting. When a study was carried out on American college students, it found that 63% of the women were on a diet as opposed to only 16% of the men. However, a large percentage of the men were concerned about being too small and 28% were trying to gain weight, often by bodybuilding methods. The evidence suggests that exercise related illnesses such as muscle dysmorphia are far more common amongst men than women.

Studies have begun to show that bodybuilders share many of the same problems as eating disordered patients. Some have developed muscle dysmorphia or 'reverse anorexia' as it is now often called. This is a condition in which the sufferer feels they can never be large enough. Although they can actually be very muscular, they are convinced that they are small and fragile. These men may increase their protein intake by 20 to 30 times that which is normal and this is very dangerous.

Body Image Problems Can Go Unnoticed

It is becoming more obvious that men feel a need to have a muscular body and equate thinness with weakness and frailty. A study of US college males found that when men were asked to pick their ideal body type, they chose a picture showing a man with approximately 28 pounds more muscle than they had on their own bodies.

Of course there are large numbers of men who do not have traditionally muscular bodies and who do not feel a strong desire to bodybuild. These men can often be left feeling inadequate and with a strong hatred for their own body. It can cause them to strive for a different shape—a lean, toned body. However, this is when problems can develop. Coupled with an already low self-esteem, these young men can take their dieting or exercise routine to an extreme and an eating disorder can result.

Often body image obsessions go unnoticed if the young man appears healthy and is engaging in what we see as healthy behaviours—exercising and watching his diet. While working out regularly is healthy, excessive exercise can be extremely damaging, especially if it is done to try and calm body image fears.

Some Sports Have a Greater Eating-Disorder Risk

Men have been found to be more at risk of developing an eating disorder if they participate in certain jobs or sports that have weight restrictions, such as wrestling, bodybuilding, swimming, horse racing and gymnastics.

It has been discovered that 8% of male athletes in Norway suffer from some kind of eating disorder. Another survey found that when they questioned athletes in the sports of boxing, weight-lifting, karate, wrestling and judo they found that 82% had used unhealthy methods such as laxatives, diuretics or diet pills to try and control their weight.

Runners are also at an increased risk of developing eating related problems. The National Runners' Survey on Dieting and Eating found that 21% of the men who answered the questionnaire were terrified of gaining weight. In other studies, it was discovered that they also seemed to have a preoccupation with food similar to that of an anorexia sufferer. They would strive to constantly lower their percentage of body fat, even when this was already very low. Many had lost 25% of their original weight and showed a relentless pursuit of thinness as well as often having a disturbed body image.

A condition known as 'Anorexia athletica' has recently been diagnosed and is specific to athletes. It is characterised by several features similar to Anorexia nervosa but without the self-starvation practises. Their severe weight loss is instead brought about by prolonged and excessive exercising.

Jockeys are also known to use many different methods of weight control prior to a race. Food restriction, excessive sauna usage, laxative and diuretic abuse, appetite suppressants, excessive exercise and self-induced vomiting can cause them to lose up to 7 lbs. in fourteen hours. All of these practices are extremely dangerous and very detrimental to their health.

Some other professions that may cause participants to be more vulnerable to eating disorders are modelling, dancing and being a flight attendant since these all necessitate weight limitations.

Preventing Eating Disorders in Men

The key to prevention for eating disorders is awareness. Parents, teachers, doctors and friends need to be conscious of potential problems in boys and men. There are certain clear warning signs:

- Changes in a person's weight.
- Mood swings—people with eating disorders frequently experience serious and prolonged depression. They often become withdrawn and can spend long periods of time on their own.
- A preoccupation with dieting and food.

Men are traditionally more emotionally withdrawn than women and this means they often find it very difficult to discuss their feelings. Men have specifically stated that they found it impossible to talk with their peers about their eating problems. They commented that the 'macho' culture meant that they were afraid their friends would think them 'weak' or 'feminine' and that they would lose all their respect.

This is another reason why it is of vital importance to men that they can access good treatment services and talk with sympathetic professionals.

FIVE

Brain Chemistry and Genetics Play a Primary Role in Eating Disorders

Mia Prensky

> Mia Prensky is a PhD student in the Department of Spanish and Portuguese at Princeton University and is a longtime bulimia sufferer. In the following viewpoint Prensky states that multiple factors influence eating disorders but argues that genetics and brain chemistry are the most important. She makes her case with references to a number of scientific studies suggesting a connection between abnormally high or low levels of brain chemicals (neurotransmitters) and the eating disorders anorexia and bulimia. She says that very low or high levels of serotonin (an important neurotransmitter) result in particular emotional and psychological problems that are typical of anorexia and bulimia. Prensky argues that those with eating disorders may attempt to feel better by restricting or bingeing on food because such behaviors increase or decrease serotonin levels, thus changing their mood.

As a long time sufferer of bulimia nervosa, an eating disorder characterized by episodes of bingeing on food followed by purging either through the use of self-induced vomiting or by

Mia Prensky, "Bulimia on the Brain," Mia Prensky's Bryn Mawr College Blog, April 18, 2007. Reproduced by permission of the author.

the abuse of laxatives and/or exercise, often including episodes of self-starvation, I have struggled with the negative stereotypes that insist on eating disorders as being the result of vanity, the desire to be thin, a characteristic highly promoted in our culture as a key element to feminine beauty and attractiveness. While social and environmental factors cannot be discarded as playing a crucial role in the development and perpetuation of eating disorders, resulting in abnormal and often extremely dangerous extremes as an attempt to control weight, we must take into consideration the other factors, such as abnormal brain chemistry and genetics, that are now shown to influence and even predispose the development and persistence of eating disorders in certain individuals.

Media and Culture Alone Do Not Explain Eating Disorders

While I do not deny the influence of media and culture on eating disorders, my own personal experience has led me to strongly believe that eating disorders such as bulimia nervosa have much less to do with body image, but rather something deep-rooted in the self, in the psychological make-up of the sufferer, something that drives the individual to pursue unhealthy, self-medicating coping skills as an attempt to ease whatever coexisting psychological illness, such as depression, anxiety, suicidal tendencies, a history of drug and/or alcohol abuse and/or obsessive-compulsive disorder. Bulimia is estimated to affect 3% of women in the United States, most of whom experience the onset of the disease during adolescence. While it is clear that all women are exposed to the cultural pressure to be thin and beautiful, only a very small percentage of women develop eating disorders, suggesting that there is something quite different about the psychological make-up of those who develop the diseases of bulimia or anorexia nervosa, the most deadly psychological illness characterized by self-starvation and extremely restricted food intake.

How Bulimia Affects Your Body

Brain
Depression, fear of gaining weight, anxiety, dizziness, shame, low self-esteem

Cheeks
Swelling, soreness

Heart
Irregular heart beat, heart muscle weakened, heart failure, low pulse and blood pressure

Mouth
Cavities, tooth enamel erosion, gum disease, teeth sensitive to hot and cold foods

Throat and Esophagus
Sore, irritated, can tear and rupture, blood in vomit

Body Fluids
Dehydration, low potassium, magnesium, and sodium

Blood
Anemia

Muscles
Fatigue

Kidneys
Problems from diuretic abuse

Stomach
Ulcers, pain, can rupture, delayed emptying

Intestines
Constipation, irregular bowel movements (BMs), bloating, diarrhea, abdominal cramping

Skin
Abrasion of knuckles, dry skin

Hormones
Irregular or absent period

Taken from: U.S. Department of Health and Human Services, www.womenshealth.gov.

Abnormal Brain Chemistry Is Strongly Implicated in Eating Disorders

Research conducted in the United States and Great Britain now suggests that chemical alterations of the brain may be a largely contributing factor in those who suffer from bulimia, particularly

Serotonin (shown here as maroon spheres) transmits nerve impulses between two brain synapses. Low serotonin levels may be a contributing factor in bulimia.

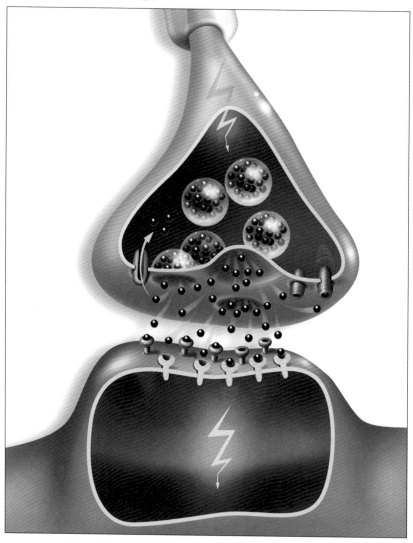

concerning the neurotransmitter serotonin. Serotonin is a neurotransmitter that acts as a messenger carrying out communication in the brain and the body. The neurotransmitter travels from one neuron along serotonergic pathways and then binds to another at a specific area of the neuron called the receptor site, and in fact disturbances in these pathways and the ability of the serotonin to bind with its corresponding receptors are shown to correlate with the presence of eating disorders. Serotonin is a neurotransmitter that helps regulate mood and is associated with many behaviors such as hunger, sleep, sexual response, impulse control, anger, aggressive behavior, anxiety, depression and perception. Abnormally low levels of serotonin correspond with increased hunger and inability to produce satiety, extreme depression, suicidal tendencies and aggression. Inversely, abnormally high levels of serotonin foster a constant state of acute anxiety (often characterized by the body's reaction to be in continual fight or flight mode), obsession with perfectionism, a constant state of feeling overwhelmed and insomnia. Other abnormalities concerning serotonin that exist in sufferers of bulimia include the persistence of the chemical alterations, including the reduction in the ability of serotonin to bind to receptors in certain brain regions following recovery from the eating disorder, as well as the continual presence of mood disorders, suggesting that coexisting psychological conditions such as depression are not a result of the bulimia, but rather a coexisting condition related to serotonin levels. Additionally, bulimic patients do not experience the normal decline of serotonin binding that occurs with aging.

Low levels of serotonin that contribute to the sense of depression are theorized to be increased during bulimic episodes of bingeing that enhance the sufferer's feeling of peace and well-being. In particular, bingeing on carbohydrates, starches and sweets are thought to increase levels of serotonin. On the other hand, the exact opposite is true for anorexics. When too much anxiety producing serotonin is present, reducing caloric intake to starvation level lowers the amount of serotonin, producing calmness and a sense of regaining control. This concept demonstrates that individuals with abnormal levels of serotonin may be subconsciously driven to eat, over-eat, or not eat at all as an attempt to increase the feeling of emotional well-being. While it is shown that irregularities in serotonin may predispose and increase vulnerability to the development of eating disorders such as bulimia, and that these irregularities persist even after recovery, it is also important to recognize that the act of starvation and purging may disrupt serotonin levels, increasing depression and anxiety, which are often considered side-effects of eating disorders as a result of vitamin deficiencies and malnutrition.

Genetic Factors in Eating Disorders

Indeed, there are individuals with elevated or reduced amounts of serotonin that do not develop eating disorders as well as the presence of eating disordered people that do not have a pre-existing condition of serotonin associated abnormalities, further suggesting the presence of other contributing factors. Genetics are now thought to play an important role in the presence of eating disorders, such as genetic predisposition to serotonin abnormalities that can run in families. It is thought that a high percentage of eating disorder patients have parents with some kind of undiagnosed anxiety or compulsive behavior disorder, while research conducted by Dr. Walter Kaye of the University of Pittsburgh, who set up an international study to see if eating disorders run in the family, showed that 10% of his anorexic and bulimic patients also had a relative with an eating disorder.

Genetic studies with relation to eating disorders have also been conducted at the Maudsley Hospital in London, focusing mainly on the serotonin system. The study involved examining the whole human genome as an attempt to find the genes that may cause anorexia, and because of the known effect of serotonin on appetite and eating, the research team investigated the 5HT2A serotonin receptor which has been shown to be involved in the regulation in feeding, and drugs that block this receptor cause weight gain. Variations in this gene for serotonin receptors were found in anorexic patients, and in fact the anorexic women were shown to be twice as likely to have the variant gene than women without eating disorders. Another discovery that demonstrates the potential of genetics to influence eating disorders is the debunking of the stereotype that eating disorders only exist in Western countries, those influenced by the culture of thinness.

An Eating Disorder Is Not the Fault of the Sufferer

Even in cultures that embrace big women as being beautiful, anorexia has been known to exist. Dr. Hans Hook conducted research in the Caribbean island of Curaçao, one such culture where fat is considered attractive. His investigation found that out of 144, 000 cases that were examined for the presence of eating disorders, 291 cases were scrutinized in detail and he was able to definitively confirm eight cases of anorexia nervosa that existed in this small population. The ratio of incidence of anorexia in Curaçao was equal to that of Europe, indicating that eating disorders exist in a cross-section of cultures in proportionate amounts, regardless of societal influences.

These investigations and studies that prove the chemical and genetic components to eating disorders such as bulimia are great strides towards the understanding and acceptance of eating disorders as a psychological disease, devaluing and disproving many of the wide-spread associated pejorative views of eating disorders as being an obsession with perfection and thinness. As long as society continues to be open-minded about the causes and reasons behind the stigmatized conditions of bulimia and anorexia, hopefully more sufferers will come forward to seek help and treatment, leaving behind the shame of their disorder. I have accepted that there are many factors that contribute to my condition of bulimia, and although I am in recovery and have successfully sought treatment, which I encourage other sufferers to do, I am relieved to know that this disease is not my fault, rather a complex combination of cultural influences, but more importantly those of genetics and brain chemistry.

SIX

Eating Disorders Are Influenced by a Variety of Factors

Something Fishy

Something Fishy is a pro-recovery Web site that has been operating since 1995 to help those suffering from anorexia, bulimia, compulsive overeating, and binge-eating disorder. In the following viewpoint the authors state that recent research shows some people may have a genetic predisposition to eating disorders, meaning their genes make them more likely to develop such a disorder by causing them to produce either too little, or too much, serotonin (a chemical messenger in the brain and body). However, they also state that some people with eating disorders do not have a genetic predisposition, and others with very low or high serotonin levels do not develop such disorders. They argue that, although unbalanced serotonin levels or genetic problems may sometimes play a role in the development of eating disorders, emotional issues, behavior, and a person's family and social environment are equally important and must be taken into account.

A great deal of research in recent years has indicated that there may be genetic factors that contribute to the onset of an Eating Disorder. This is not to say that emotional, behavioral and environmental reasons do not play significant roles, but that for some, there may be a genetic predisposition to the development of Anorexia, Bulimia or Compulsive Overeating.

One study by doctors at the Maudsley Hospital in London suggested that people with Anorexia were twice as likely to have variations in the gene for serotonin receptors, part of which helps to determine appetite. Because of an overproduction of serotonin, it is possible that those with Anorexia are in a continual state of feeling acute stress—as in the fight or flight response—creating an overwhelming and constant sense of anxiety.

Another study by Dr. Walter Kaye, of the University of Pittsburgh, examined a number of recovered Bulimia patients. They were monitored for persistent behavior disturbances and levels of serotonin, dopamine and norepinephrine. His team found that, compared to people with no history of Bulimia, the recovered individuals still had abnormal serotonin levels, with overall more negative moods, and obsessions with perfectionism and exactness. The levels of the other brain chemicals, dopamine and norephinephrine, were normal in comparison.

The Role of Serotonin

Serotonin (ser-oh-TOH-nin) is a neurotransmitter, a group of chemical messengers that carry out communication in the brain and body. The messengers travel from one neuron (or nerve cell) to others that act as receivers, where they attach to a specific area called a receptor site. This union, like a key fitting into a lock, triggers signals that either allow or prevent a message to be passed on to other cells. Since the discovery of serotonin in the 1950s, researchers are finding evidence that one of its roles is to mediate emotions and judgment.

Serotonin is involved in many behaviors such as hunger, sleep, sexual response, impulse control, aggressive behavior and anger, depression, anxiety and perception. Abnormally low levels of serotonin might be found in someone who is suicidal, who is particularly aggressive towards others, or a person who is extremely depressed. High levels of serotonin may be found in a person who is in a constant state of anxiety, has a tendency to be over-exacting in completing tasks, who suffers insomnia, or who has a tendency to feel overly stimulated by their surroundings (overwhelmed).

Implications for Eating Disorders

Low levels of serotonin, which could contribute to a person's sense of depression, are in theory increased during episodes of bingeing, making the person actually feel better. As theorized, bingeing on sweets, starches or carbohydrates would increase serotonin and produce a sense of well-being.

The exact opposite would be true in conjunction with self-starvation or restriction. If too much serotonin is present, this may create a sense of perpetual anxiety, and in theory, by reducing the intake of calories to starvation level, the result would be a calming or sense of regaining control.

In other words, those with low or high levels of serotonin may feel "driven" towards eating or not eating as they consciously or subconsciously realize it actually makes them feel better emotionally, because of a physical response in their brain.

It is very important to note that the act of restricting, and bingeing (with or without purging) can also lead to a disruption in serotonin levels, thus contributing to an already existing problem, or creating a completely new one to deal with. This can lead to depression and anxiety, which are known side effects of malnutrition and vitamin deficiencies, both for undereaters and overeaters.

In addition to Depression and Anxiety, abnormal serotonin levels have been found in people with other mental illness, such as Obsessive Compulsive Disorder, Bipolar Disorder, Borderline Personality Disorder, and Attention Deficit/Hyperactivity Disorder (ADHD), all of which can, for some, co-exist with an Eating Disorder. Studies also suggest that there are genetic predispositions to serotonin disruptions, that appear to run in some families.

Other Significant Factors

While all of the genetic studies and biological predispositions may be important to understand, it is essential to realize that there are people who live with too much or too little serotonin who do not

Causes of Eating Disorders Are Multiple and Complex

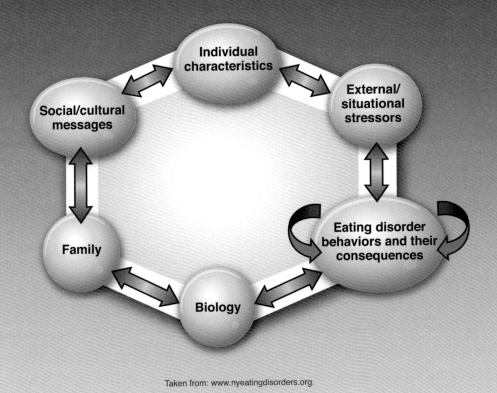

Taken from: www.nyeatingdisorders.org.

develop an Eating Disorder. It is also important to note that there are people who develop an Eating Disorder who have no corresponding predisposition. While there may be genes that play a role in the level of serotonin within our brains (for some people), the emphasis on emotional, behavioral and environmental factors cannot and should not be dismissed. For some, low or high levels of serotonin may make a person predisposed to relying on food as a way to control how they feel, but that doesn't elimate all of the non-biological possibilities.

One way to look at this is to examine a child with Attention Deficit Disorder (ADD) that has a parent with ADD. The family environment may be very chaotic, in part due to the way they are hard-wired, but also because of an inability to cope effectively with the ADD. These behavioral patterns, as well as a sense of instability in the environment, are as much a contribution to the way the child learns to cope, as is the genetic influence of ADD. One doctor we spoke with said, "I find that a really high percentage of the [eating-disorders] clients I work with have parents with some kind of undiagnosed anxiety or compulsive behavior type. They may learn how to have these behaviors themselves simply by living in such an environment. Only when they grow up and leave the home do they even have the opportunity to see that what they learned may be dysfunctional."

Medications such as selective serotonin reuptake inhibitors, or SSRIs, can help control serotonin levels, which enables patients to respond to treatment more effectively.

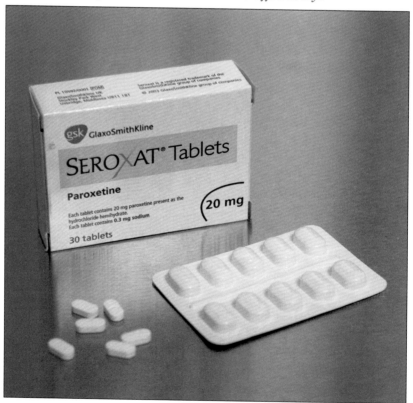

As stressed above there are many things that may play a role in the onset of an Eating Disorder: Family environments, the way a person was taught to [and how they] cope with their emotions, how they were taught to [and how they] communicate, their general sense of self-esteem, and possible issues of physical, emotional or sexual abuse. Another factor may be a history of addiction to drugs or alcohol in a family, and the effect it may play both genetically and environmentally. The problems each person faces, the way they cope, the reasons for continuing to hurt or punish themselves, and the way they feel are all critical issues that cannot be tossed aside.

Each Eating Disorder Sufferer Is an Individual

Keep in mind, low levels of serotonin have been discovered in some alcoholics as well, but not everyone with a low level of serotonin would become an alcoholic, stressing the point that there are other contributing factors.

Though serotonin may play a role in feeling depressed or overly anxious, it is not the only reason people suffer from depression or anxiety, nor the only reason they may develop an Eating Disorder. It may, for some, be an important piece to the puzzle, but isn't by itself a complete picture.

> Although no one can yet say for certain, new science is offering tantalizing clues. Doctors now compare anorexia to alcoholism and depression, potentially fatal diseases that may be set off by environmental factors such as stress or trauma, but have their roots in a complex combination of genes and brain chemistry. In other words, many kids are affected by pressure-cooker school environments and a culture of thinness promoted by magazines and music videos, but most of them don't secretly scrape their dinner into the garbage. The environment "pulls the trigger," says Cynthia Bulik, director of the eating-disorder program at the University of North Carolina at Chapel Hill. "But it's a child's latent vulnerabilities that 'load the gun.'"[1]

Keeping the big picture in mind it may be useful to be aware of how serotonin levels affect each particular person when it comes to their course of treatment. Medications such as SSRIs (selective serotonin reuptake inhibitors) can help to control levels of serotonin and assist patients in responding more positively to therapy and treatment . . . but there is no "magic pill." Each individual will ultimately respond best when they can find a therapist and treatment team that can address all issues.

Each Eating Disorder sufferer is an individual. Some may respond to medication, some may not, and some may not wish to take it at all. Some may endure "the serotonin roller coaster ride" while trying to find the healthy middle-ground in which the medication becomes effective. It is important for those in recovery, along with their doctors and therapists, to keep all of this in mind, communicate about what is going on, and to remain patient through the process.

Note

1. *Newsweek*, "Fighting Anorexia: No One to Blame," December 2005.

SEVEN

Eating Disorders Are a Spiritual Crisis

Courtney E. Martin

Courtney E. Martin is a journalist, senior correspondent for the *American Prospect*, and author of *Perfect Girls, Starving Daughters: How the Quest for Perfection Is Harming Young Women*. In the following viewpoint Martin suggests that a lack of healthy religion or spirituality in the lives of girls growing up today, combined with an overemphasis on success, leads many vulnerable young women to focus on "perfecting" their bodies as a substitute for a fundamental sense of divinity. Martin states that there is too much emphasis on ambition, with even community service being done to improve college applications. She argues that what is needed is a return to spiritual values that support a healthy self-image in women.

Worried talk about the next generation of high-achieving, health-neglecting "perfect girls" is everywhere.

Girls Inc. just published [in 2006] the results of its depressing, nationwide survey called "The Supergirl Dilemma," which reveals that girls' obsession with thinness has gotten significantly worse in the past six years. Despite the efforts of the Dove's Campaign for Real Beauty—well-intentioned, though undeniably market-driven—and Love Your Body Day events sweeping every school from San Francisco to Syracuse, 90 percent of teenage girls think they are overweight today, compared with 24 percent in 1995, according to a recent ELLEgirl survey.

So what gives? Is it our celebrity-obsessed, extreme makeover culture? Is it the newest version of the age-old story of dysfunctional family relationships? Is it peer pressure—mean girls critiquing one another's every lunchtime indiscretion? Is it the $30 billion a year diet industry?

Genuine Spirituality Is Missing from Modern Life

It is, in truth, all of the above. But there is also another profoundly important—yet little noticed—dynamic at work in the anxious, achievement-oriented lives of America's perfect girls: They have a sometimes deadly, often destructive, lack of faith.

So many perfect girls were raised entirely without organized religion, and the majority of the rest of us—I reluctantly admit to my own membership in the perfect girl club—experienced "spirituality" only in the form of mandatory holiday services with a big-haired grandmother or unconscionably elaborate and expensive bat mitvah parties, where everything but the Torah is emphasized.

Overlay our dearth of spiritual exploration with our excess of training in ambition—never mind SAT [Scholastic Aptitude Test] prep courses; today, even community service is linked to college application brownie points—and you have a generation of godless girls. We were raised largely without a fundamental sense of divinity. In fact, our worth in the world has always been tied to our looks, grades, and gifts—not the amazing miracle of mere existence.

Perfecting the Body as a Religious Obsession

In this climate, we feel perpetually called to perfect our own "body projects"—the term used by historian Joan Jacob Brumberg. Thinness and achievement stand in for the qualities of kindness and humility. We think that our perfect bodies—not God's grace or good works—will get us into heaven. We have no deeply held

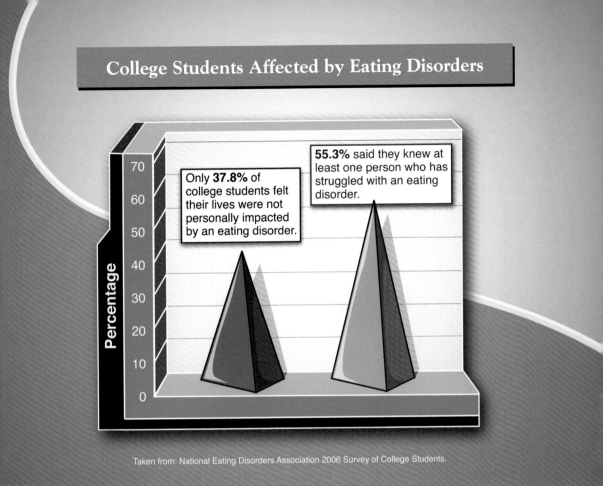

College Students Affected by Eating Disorders

Only **37.8%** of college students felt their lives were not personally impacted by an eating disorder.

55.3% said they knew at least one person who has struggled with an eating disorder.

Percentage

70
60
50
40
30
20
10
0

Taken from: National Eating Disorders Association 2006 Survey of College Students.

sense of our own divinity, so we chase after some unattainable ideal. Perfect girls, as a result, feel they are never enough. Never disciplined enough. Never accomplished enough. Never thin enough.

The worst of this can be seen in the frightening websites that purport to be support groups for girls with anorexia and bulimia. Such sites claim that these two disorders are a religion, not a disease, and pray to false gods named after them: Ana and Mia. Though highly deluded and dangerously ill, girls who frequent these sites have taken the black hole at their centers and filled it with an obsessive faith in the power and purity of thinness. In essence, they are crying out to our godless culture, showing us just how damaged a child can be who is thrown to the wolves of advertising and amoral media without any spiritual armor.

Spiritual Values for Those with Eating Disorders

I'm not calling for a return to conservative religion or restricting dogma. I'm envisioning an inspired movement toward community where girls are nourished with dinner-table conversations about the values of kindness and charity; where girls undergoing

The author says, in essence, that girls today are spiritually malnourished and would do well to heed Buddha's message about the importance of loving oneself.

puberty are encouraged to embrace the miraculous, complex, and perfectly imperfect bodies they possess; and where girls can find inspiration—not condemnation—in religious texts.

For starters, the Bible has something to teach the perfect girl who calculates beauty in terms of pounds and dress sizes: "Your beauty should not come from outward adornment. . . . Instead, it should be that of your inner self, the unfading beauty of a gentle and quiet spirit, which is of great worth in God's sight" (I Peter 3:3,4). (New International Version)

And Buddha, the man often portrayed as blissful with his belly, has a paradigm-shifting message for the average American woman accustomed to self-hate: "You, yourself, as much as anybody in the entire universe, deserve your love and affection."

In the age of the skeletal celebrity-filled *US Weekly* and shrill sound bite commentators such as Ann Coulter, these are the kinds of deep reflections and recommendations we perfect girls need most.

A supermom of an elite college hopeful told *New York Times* reporter Sara Rimer, "You just hope your child doesn't have anorexia of the soul." While she is spot on in her fears, she seems woefully shortsighted about her responsibilities. It is we, all of us, who have the power to resurrect a society that values spirit above skinniness. We have to start doing it—one prayer, one family hike, one heart-to-heart discussion about what really matters—at a time.

EIGHT

Models and Actresses Contribute to Poor Self-Image Among Girls

Uttara Manohar

Uttara Manohar is a writer and a student at Ohio State University studying mass communication. In the following viewpoint Manohar states that overly skinny actresses and models are far too common in the media. She discusses several common eating disorders (anorexia, bulimia, and compulsive overeating) and argues that distorted media depictions and expectations contribute to these disorders. Manohar claims that society is ready for change in this area and encourages the media to recognize this and to start portraying healthier women and a greater diversity of female beauty.

Media plays an important role in influencing people's opinions and choices. Especially in terms of body images, the media has created certain ideal body images, which are continuously being flashed via various mass media. The magazines, newspapers, television, radio as well as the Internet are full of images of slim and slender models, which are often perceived as the most-sought-after or desirable body images. Most of the celebrities seem to be flaunting their chiseled bodies and flat stomachs and although some of them might be actually the result of strenuous workouts and healthy diets—there are [a] huge number of models that are plain anorexic.

The Media's Overemphasis on
Skinny Models and Actresses

Why aren't there enough voluptuous models on the ramp? Why does a television advertisement for some toothpaste commercial have to be a size zero model? Why is the petite size the most

According to the author, the mass media continues to propagate images of impossibly thin women, setting an unattainable standard for most women and causing them to be insecure about their bodies.

sought-after size? Why do programs about celebrity news criticize a particular celebrity when he/she gains a few extra pounds? Ever wondered about the messages that the media is sending out with these trends? Does an average teenager know what body mass index is? Does she/he know that there is a body type that exists between being skinny and being overweight?

Although there are increasing numbers of people who are propagating the benefits of a healthy body and warning people about the ill-effects of unhealthy body weights, a large number of media messages just can't seem to shift the focus from slim and slender bodies to healthier body images. Although there might be people who would want to cite the references of plus-size models, when was the last time you saw a huge number of voluptuous models walking for the biggies? Or when was the last time you saw a beauty pageant contestant who didn't have a slender figure?

Media's influence has resulted in creation of ideal body images, which are almost impossible to achieve for each and everyone. Failed attempts at reducing weight and getting skinnier tend to result in unhealthy eating disorders, which culminate in severe medical conditions and finally affect the overall health of the person. There are thousands of teenage girls who have fallen prey to these trends and have gone through traumatic experiences, which led to a physical as well as a psychological imbalance.

Commonly Observed Eating Disorders

Although toned bodies and petite sizes seem to be the most sought-after assets for millions of young girls out there, not everyone is ready to adopt the healthy road to fitness. A large number of the victims of eating disorders are young girls and women who are constantly running after a mirage of petite sizes rather than aiming for health and fitness. Here are some of the eating disorders that are commonly observed:

Anorexia: Anorexia nervosa is a psychological disorder, which is characterized by distorted perceptions of the body image and persistent fear of weight gain, which results in self-starvation and an extreme weight loss. A large number of teenage girls fall prey to the portrayal of ideal body images on the media and in an attempt to attain this body image, they reduce their food intake by going on dangerous crash diets, which result in conditions like anorexia.

Bulimia: Bulimia nervosa, which is commonly referred to as bulimia, is a psychological condition and an eating disorder which is marked by binge eating, followed by guilt and intentional purging to compensate for the binge eating. Purging can be by means of vomiting, fasting, use of laxatives, enemas or even diuretics. Women between ages 16–40 constitute the majority of people suffering from this eating disorder.

Compulsive Overeating: Compulsive overeating or food addiction is an eating disorder which is marked by frequent episodes of binge eating, where a person cannot exercise control over the intake of food. However, in this disorder the person does not try and purge the food, but instead tends to keep on eating even when he/she is not hungry. Compulsive overeating usually leads to obesity since the person uses food for comfort.

Effects of Media on Body Image Perception

In addition to these eating disorders, there are other disorders like body dysmorphic disorder, which tend to distort perceptions about self body image. The media creates a tremendous hype about the beautiful celebrities who have bodies which are touted as the most desirable looks or body images. There are people who are ready to go under the knife to look good. People are resorting to cosmetic surgeries to have Jennifer Anniston's nose or Angelina Jolie's lips without giving it a second thought! The media is giving out the wrong messages no doubt, but then it is also the passive blind-followers of media trends that are at fault. Communication schools have spotted this issue and are studying the various aspects of media effects on body image perception.

'You have potential, but you need to lose some weight', cartoon by Mike Artell. www.Cartoon Stock.com.

A large number of research projects are focused on studying the effects of media on adolescents' body image distortions. A large number of studies in this area have cited a relationship between fashion magazine reading and eating disorders and even television viewing and body dissatisfaction, which is a clear indicator of the fact that media does play an influential role and is one of the major causes for a large number of people who are suffering from eating disorders. Parental mediation and media literacy seem to be some of the possible solutions which have been suggested to tackle this problem.

On a personal level, what you can do is to try and redefine your outlook towards perceiving ideal body images and knowing what works the best for your body type. At the same time let us hope that the media awakens to the fact that role models and celebrities are people that we want to relate to and look up to. The society is ready to accept full-figured models that are healthy rather than being skinny and famished. There are a large number of plus-size models [who are] struggling to make their mark in the fashion industry but have limited opportunities. There are several teenagers who are recovering from their bulimic and anorexic lifestyles and are ready to embrace a healthy lifestyle. A majority of the audiences are gradually accepting the healthy body image portrayal, but is the media ready to shift the focus from size zero?

NINE

Thin Actresses and Models Do Not Make Girls Anorexic

Fred Schwarz

Fred Schwarz is a deputy managing editor at the *National Review*. In the following viewpoint Schwarz argues that the belief that the media and culture cause eating disorders is wrong and that efforts to ban skinny models are misguided. He discusses cases of anorexia occurring historically and in places where thinness is not highly valued (as it is in modern American society), arguing that if eating disorders occur in cultures that do not see extreme thinness as valuable, then they cannot be caused by culture or the media in these countries. He also briefly discusses several theories about the causes of eating disorders, all of which claim some physical problem is the underlying issue. Schwarz contends that changing the media will not help reduce eating disorders and that attempts to portray a greater variety of female body types in the media have failed because both male and female viewers "like beautiful actresses rather than healthy ones."

What causes anorexia nervosa, the terrible mental illness whose victims (mostly young women) starve themselves, sometimes to death? To many observers, the answer is clear: Hollywood, Madison Avenue [advertising center in New York

City], and Seventh Avenue [center of New York City's fashion industry]. Film and television actresses are impossibly thin; advertisers hawk an endless profusion of diet products and banish average-looking people from their commercials; the fashion industry recruits tall, scrawny teenagers as its models and tosses them aside if they become too womanly. When girls and young women are constantly bombarded with thin-is-beautiful messages, is it any wonder that some of them overreact?

Christy Greenleaf, assistant professor of kinesiology, health promotion, and recreation at the University of North Texas, doesn't think so. She has written: "Girls and women, in our society, are socialized to value physical appearance and an ultra-thin beauty that rarely occurs naturally and to pursue that ultra-thin physique at any cost. Research demonstrates that poor body image and disordered eating attitudes are associated with internalizing the mediated (i.e., commodified, airbrushed) bodies that dominate the fashion industry." The narrative is a plausible one, and it fits a familiar template: Big business uses mass media to destroy consumers' health by creating harmful desires. Yet there are large parts of it that don't hold up.

Anorexia in Historical Times

In the first place, anorexia is not in any way an artifact of our modern, weight-obsessed society. [English philosopher] Thomas Hobbes wrote about it in the 1680s. A 1987 study showed that anorexia in the United States increased throughout the 19th century and peaked around 1900, when chorus girls were voluptuous and the boyish flapper look was still two decades away. A similar historical pattern has been found for eating disorders in France. Some interplay of genetic and environmental factors may be at work in these cases, or they may have resulted from the common pattern in medicine of certain diagnoses' rising and falling in popularity. But it's clear that none of these outbreaks can be attributed to the late-20th- and early-21st-century emphasis on skinniness.

Anorexia is not just a modern phenomenon. English philosopher Thomas Hobbes wrote about it in the late seventeenth century.

There are plenty of other examples. The medical historian I.S.L. Loudon has identified chlorosis, the 19th-century "virgin's disease," with anorexia and shown that diagnoses of it reached "epidemic proportions" in Victorian England before disappearing completely between 1900 and 1920. A pair of Dutch historians have traced the practice of severe self-starvation all the way back to the early Christians and described the various explanations that were offered for it over the centuries (holiness, witchcraft, demonic possession, miracles, various nervous or emotional disturbances) before a newly scientific medical profession defined it as an illness in the mid-19th century.

All these statistics must be taken as rough indications only. Eating-disorder rates, like those for most psychiatric illnesses, are notoriously slippery, since the conditions are so hard to pin down. Journalists sometimes say that anorexia rates have been increasing for decades, as Americans' lives have become more media-saturated; one source reports that anorexia in young adult females has tripled over the past 40 years. This is a case of the common phenomenon in which growing awareness of a condition leads to increased diagnosis of it, even when there is no real increase in its prevalence. Researchers who have carefully studied the data conclude that there has been no significant change in the rate of anorexia in America since at least the mid-20th century.

A Global Phenomenon

Moreover, while it's tempting to blame America's appearance-obsessed culture for the plight of its self-starving daughters, anorexia is a global phenomenon. A 2001 article reviewed the extensive literature on eating disorders among residents of Europe, Asia, Africa, the Middle East, and Australia. In some regions, the reported rates of anorexia were several times that of the United States (though, as above, such figures must be taken with caution). In a case of political correctness attacking itself, one researcher says those who attribute anorexia to media sexism are being ethnocentric: "The biomedical definition of anorexia nervosa emphasizes fat-phobia. . . . However, evidence exists that suggests anorexia nervosa can exist without the Western fear of fatness and that this culturally biased view of anorexia nervosa may obscure health care professionals' understanding of a patient's own cultural reasons for self-starvation."

Anorexia Has Physical Roots

If it isn't skinny models, what's the cause? In the last dozen years or so, scientists have linked anorexia to many different physiological conditions: high levels of estrogen in the womb; low levels of serotonin in the brain; a genetic mutation; overactivity by dopamine receptors; a general tendency toward anxiety and obsessionality; high age at menarche [start of menstruation]; elevated amounts of a mysterious peptide [part of a protein in the body] called CART; autism (which is underdiagnosed in girls, perhaps because it sometimes manifests itself in the form of eating disorders); premature birth or other birth complications; irregular activity in the insular cortex of the brain; posttraumatic stress disorder; an autoimmune disorder affecting the hypothalamus and pituitary gland; variations in the structure of the anterior ventral striatum (the brain region responsible for emotional responses); and even being born in June (seriously—one theory is that a winter-type disease in the mother at a certain vulnerable point during the pregnancy is responsible). Some of these causes may overlap with one another, but biomedical researchers are virtually unanimous that anorexia has physical roots, though the mechanism remains poorly understood.

Might these physiological factors be what makes one susceptible to anorexia, but cultural images are what sets it off? Walter Kaye, a psychiatry professor at [the University of California at] San Diego, has suggested such a mechanism: "Less than half of 1 percent of all women develop anorexia nervosa, which indicates to us that societal pressure alone isn't enough to cause someone to develop this disease. Our research has found that genes seem to play a substantial role in determining who is vulnerable to developing an eating disorder. However, the societal pressure isn't irrelevant; it may be the environmental trigger that releases a person's genetic risk."

Maybe, but probably not. As noted above, anorexia has flourished in many times and places with no mass media and no ideal of thinness. Anorexia could be just another manifestation of self-destructiveness, like slashing one's wrists. It could stem from some cause unrelated to body image, such as disgust with the processes of digestion and elimination (as well as menstruation, which often ceases in long-term anorexics). Psychiatrists believe that many anorexic women want to reverse the effects of puberty, such as breasts and hips, and while most of today's film and television sex symbols are indeed slender, they rarely lack for breasts and hips.

Changing the Media Is Not the Answer

Despite the uncertain connection, some observers still think the media need to change their act. Professor Greenleaf has suggested: "A potentially healthier approach is to include [in advertising] a variety of body shapes and sizes (as opposed to idealizing only one physique). Healthy bodies come in all shapes and sizes—and health is what should be valued, which may not fit with the fashion industry's emphasis on ultra-thin beauty."

The suggestion is not outlandish. Many advertisers and fashion magazines have, in fact, tried using "a variety of body shapes and sizes" among their models—once. It makes a decent publicity gimmick, but there's a reason they always go back to slender models: Clothes look better on them. (Also, it usually isn't practical to custom-sew garments for individual models, so clothing samples are made for a standard size 6.) And for some reason, viewers of films and television, male and female, tend to like beautiful actresses rather than healthy ones—not to mention the common observation that "the camera adds ten pounds."

If increasing the labor pool for models and actresses by including heftier ones yielded equally good results, the industries in question would have done it long ago. Why deal with a bunch of stuck-up teenagers if you don't have to? If media and fashion conglomerates really do dictate our image of the ideal female, why don't they manipulate us into going crazy for plumpish housewives instead? And even if it's true that media images make some people weight-conscious, the benefits must easily exceed the costs, since obesity is a much greater problem in America than anorexia.

Calls for Bans on Skinny Models Are Misguided

Nonetheless, some lawmakers are calling for bans on skinny models. Madrid and Milan have prohibited those with a body-mass index lower than 18 from their fashion shows. (Body-mass index is the weight in kilograms divided by the square of the height in meters. A BMI of 18 is considered the low end of the normal range, but you wouldn't expect models as a group to have "normal" physiques, any more than you would expect it from football players.) Similar bans have been proposed in Quebec, London, New York City, New York State, and France's national assembly. The main goal of these bills, which began to be introduced after several models starved themselves to death, is supposedly to reduce anorexia within the industry, though proponents always invoke the baleful effects that waif-like models have on society as a whole. Yet this assumes that self-starvation is a willful choice

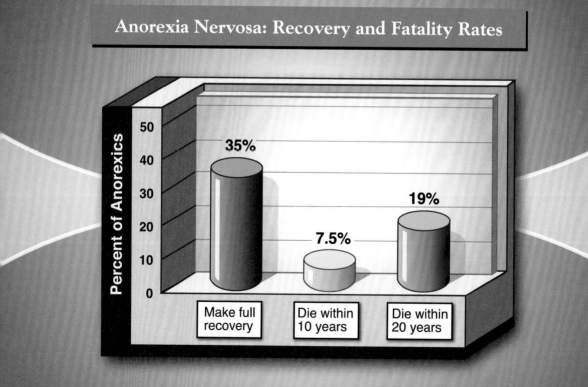

Taken from: Aleks Cherednichenko, "Eating Disorders Affect More than Half of U.S. Population," *Daily Barometer*, February 26, 2008, South Carolina Department of Mental Health.

that anorexics will abandon if given the proper incentive, when in fact it is a mental illness that for centuries has proven stubbornly impervious to rational arguments.

Anorexia is a dreadful disease, and still poorly understood. If the growing scientific knowledge about it can be pieced together, we may eventually learn to identify, prevent, treat, and possibly cure it. But political activists do not help its sufferers when they oversimplify a complicated condition and blame it on their stock assortment of evil forces in American society.

TEN

"Pro-Ana" Web Sites Resemble Cults

Matthew Tiemeyer

Matthew Tiemeyer is a licensed counselor with a private practice in Seattle, specializing in the treatment of eating disorders, sexual abuse, and relationship issues. In the following viewpoint Tiemeyer argues that "pro-ana nation"—people who believe that eating disorders are positive—are dangerously cultlike. Although he says that such Web sites provide needed emotional support, he believes they reinforce disordered eating and encourage social isolation. He argues that these sites have disturbing similarities to cults; for example, the eating disorder is seen as the only way to live, and since "no one else will understand," sufferers isolate themselves from family and friends. The author says the sites differ from cults in some ways, but the similarities need to be taken into account—in particular, since it is very difficult to leave an eating disorder behind, those who wish to recover need multiple treatment providers as well as healthy emotional connections to help them look forward rather than return to past dysfunctional patterns.

Yes, it's a provocative thought. "Pro-ana nation," the collective group of those who believe that eating disorders are positive, certainly has views that many of us would find odd. But a cult? It seems a bit over the top: After all, some telltale signs of a cult aren't there. There's no clear organization for those with pro-ana [pro-anorexia] views, no exalted leader who dictates what those who are pro-ana or pro-mia [in favor of bulimia] must do.

On the other hand, there are some troubling similarities between subscribers to the pro-ana view and cults. For example, cults seem like the only options for life to those who are involved.

Web Sites Promoting Anorexia or Bulimia

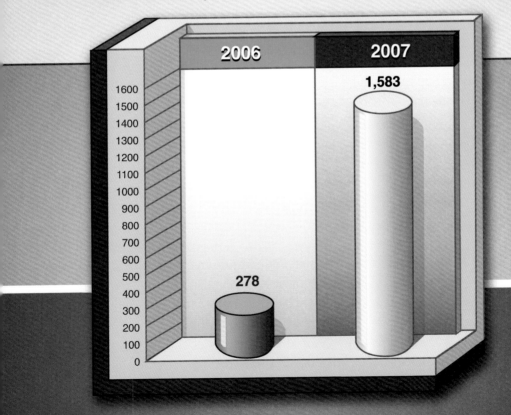

Pro-ana and Pro-mia Web sites promoting anorexia or bulimia increased 469.42 percent from 2006 to 2007.

Leaving a cult can feel like an incredible loss. There is a sense of feeling special, even "chosen," that is often present. All these exist for those with eating disorders—anorexia nervosa in particular.

Deciding whether the pro-ana community is a cult or not won't make the sites go away. But it's instructive to understand what it costs a person to enter that community, and also what it costs to get out.

How Pro-Ana Sites Benefit Users

A rare (so far) study of the behavior of those who go to pro-ana web sites investigated in depth why people view them and what they do while they're there. The mix of responses leads me to wonder whether the sites serve as a group of cult-like destinations.

Nearly 20% of respondents said that they found the pro-ana sites harmful—that they encouraged stressful competition and led to lower self-esteem. The same is true of cults, in general. Some within every cult recognize the harm that occurs. Only some of those who see, however, actually leave.

But most found the pro-ana sites helpful. These fell into two groups. The smaller group (17%) admitted that the sites helped them to continue their disordered eating. While this subgroup found the sites "helpful," it's clear that these visitors were being harmed: Eating disorders are clearly harmful. Again, bizarre (and sometimes dangerous or abusive) behaviors are common in cults, and some who practice them consider them somehow "helpful."

That leaves the only group that seems truly to benefit from pro-ana sites. The larger group of those who found the sites helpful (43%) said that the key benefit is emotional support. Visitors to pro-ana sites who participated more in chat rooms and forums generally felt more supported emotionally.

The authors suggested that this support may represent a benefit that those in the mental health field do not acknowledge. But is this brand of emotional support beneficial to this particular population? Unfortunately, there are strong reasons to believe that it isn't.

People with Eating Disorders Need Emotional Support

A key reason that pro-ana and pro-mia sites are attractive is that those with eating disorders do not easily develop relationships with others. They may have at previous times, but eating disorders tend to create isolation. Going to a pro-ana site reminds a

Anorexia sufferers tend to isolate themselves from friends and family, which can make pro-ana Web sites appealing to them.

person that she is not alone: Others know the emotions and can be "with" her as she makes choices. Since many don't understand much about eating disorders, there is relief in grouping with those who do.

Understanding this, operators of pro-ana sites provide discussion forums and chat rooms. Members provide encouragement to each other, whether it be emotional support or "accountability" to continue disordered eating behaviors.

But while many keep coming back to these sites for support, it's a support that doesn't promote emotional growth. True support enables a person to explore the world and to make hard decisions. A well-supported person feels comfortable in establishing new friendships from many places as well as maintaining the current friendships. Pro-eating disorder site visitors tend to turn more and more inward, shrinking their circles of friends. The result is that "pro-ana nation" becomes the only acceptable social outlet. Meanwhile, the exposure to disordered eating habits deepens. This is yet another red flag: Separation from past relationships, as well as past interests and pursuits, is typical of cults.

Similarities Between Pro-Ana Sites and Cults

Of course, blanketing all pro-ana sites with the "cult" label is presumptuous. So I looked up a checklist of cult behaviors. Comparing these factors (which I've paraphrased for brevity) to the dynamics of those in "pro-ana nation" reveals troubling parallels:

- *The group is excessively committed to its leader. Whatever the leader says goes.* There's no human leader manipulating pro-eating disorder people. In fact, those with anorexia are particularly independent and resist being led. But the messages the eating disorder brings are powerful. It almost always gets what it wants.

- *Mind-altering practices suppress doubts about the group and its leader.* Both restriction and the binge/purge cycle alter the mind. Chemical balance in the body changes and makes clear thought much more difficult.

- *The group is elitist, claiming a special status and purpose.* This one's only partially applicable. Those with anorexia do feel quite special and powerful (while appearing very humble). However, I can't identify some lofty larger purpose for the group.

- *The group has an us-versus-them mentality, which may cause conflict with society.* It occurs in families and also in larger groups. The eating disorder feels like the only way to live, so those who disagree seem to threaten life.

- *The leader is not accountable to any authorities.* If the eating disorder is the "leader," this applies. It can't be governed by anyone.

- *The group implies that its ends justify whatever means necessary.* Try to force a person with bulimia to stop bingeing and purging, and you'll be amazed at how intense the fight will be.

- *The leadership induces feelings of shame and/or guilt in order to influence and/or control members.* Often, this is done through peer pressure and subtle persuasion. Shame is the chief emotion underlying eating disorders. And some of the internal "persuasion" is not so subtle.

- *Being a member requires cutting ties with family and friends, and radically altering the goals and activities they had before joining.* There's no "requirement," but the ties are cut just the same.

- *Members are encouraged or required to live and/or socialize only with other group members.* The eating disorder whispers, "No one else will understand."

- *The most loyal members believe that there is no life outside the group.* Those who consider recovering think precisely these thoughts. It's the eating disorder or nothing.

How Pro-Ana Sites Differ from Cults

Yet with all the similarities between pro-eating disorder groups and cults, there are also notable differences. Here are some cult behaviors that don't seem to apply:

- *The group is preoccupied with bringing in new members.* This might be debatable, since young people are especially likely to learn about eating disorders from their friends and acquaintances (and family, for that matter). But there's no "membership drive" or requirement for growth as it exists in some cults.

- *The group is preoccupied with making money.* Realistically, participation in the group takes away time that might be otherwise spent on making income. And nobody's getting paid; mainstream advertisers aren't looking to pro-ana sites as opportunities.

- *Members are expected to devote inordinate amounts of time to the group and group-related activities.* It's not likely that someone would complain that a forum visitor just isn't spending enough time in disordered eating. Actually, there's no need: Eating disorders suck up huge amounts of time with or without encouragement from others.

Recovery Offers a Healthier Form of Support

It's unfair simply to dismiss "pro-ana nation" as a cult. Besides being inaccurate, it's an inflammatory term that may strengthen the will of those with eating disorders to stay on their current courses. It also makes it easier to forget that each person in the group is unique and that there are reasons that each eating disorder started, some of which are very painful.

But while pro-eating disorder sites may not be cults, it's naive to ignore the similarities. These parallels extend into the sometimes gut-wrenching process of moving on.

It takes resources for a person to leave a cult. There must be many voices saying what's true to counteract the cult's messages. In some cases, a person wanting to leave will need physical protection. And when life outside gets confusing, it's common for ex-cult members to be drawn back toward the situations they left. Cults eliminate a lot of choices that those who are free make routinely.

For those who wish to recover from eating disorders, multiple treatment providers are the many truthful voices. Physical "protection" is required in the form of medical support as the body reacts to more normal eating patterns. And just as cult members need support from healthy people to expand their horizons and leave behind what endangered them, those with eating disorders need solid emotional connections to avoid relapse and look forward, rather than returning to the past. Those who view pro-ana sites for "emotional support" should know that they can receive a more healthy, genuine brand of that support in the process of recovery.

ELEVEN

Family Plays an Important Role in Eating Disorder Recovery

James Lock

> James Lock is associate professor of child psychiatry and pediatrics at Stanford University School of Medicine in Stanford, California. He also directs the eating disorder program for children and adolescents at Lucile Packard Children's Hospital in Palo Alto, California. In the following viewpoint Lock describes a long history of parents being blamed for causing their child's eating disorder and being told by professionals not to be involved with their child at all during recovery. The author claims that this practice has been based on theory alone and is not supported by observation of families. He argues that actual families need to be assessed to decide what therapies are effective and states that, according to recent evidence, parents can be a very positive influence on their child's healing process.

Parents are often uncertain, and understandably so, about how to respond to their son or daughter when they develop anorexia nervosa (AN). They are confused by the symptoms, which seem at first an innocent enough exploration of dieting common to

James Lock, "Parents: Are They a Help or Hindrance in the Treatment of Anorexia?" *Brown University Child and Adolescent Behavior Letter*, vol. 22, October 2006. Copyright © 2006 Wiley Periodicals, Inc. Reproduced with permission of John Wiley & Sons, Inc.

many adolescents, but that then rapidly become startlingly bizarre and deadly. They are confused by how their child, who previously was amiable and compliant, becomes withdrawn, irritable and defiant, especially around eating. And they are particularly confused about what professionals tell them: don't get involved, let her decide, you can only make things worse.

Parents Have Been Seen as a Cause

Starting with William Gull in 1876, who observed families to be the "worst attendants" for their children suffering from AN, to Salvadore Minuchin's specific formulations characterizing such families as psychosomatic (enmeshed, overprotective, rigid and conflict avoidant), parents in particular have been regarded as likely to be the cause of the problem with few positive resources to recommend them. Thus when adolescents with AN were treated, regardless of the approach or setting, it has been common for parents and families to be excluded from care and viewed as the source of the problem.

In practice this has meant that when adolescents were treated in inpatient settings, parental visits were highly restricted. In many cases, parents were not permitted contact of any kind with their child for extended periods. Such "parentectomies" [removal of the parents] were viewed as providing an opportunity to break the pathological hold of family processes believed to have caused AN. In this same spirit, individual outpatient therapies justified the exclusion of parents often to the point of not communicating even the most basic information about medical progress. When families and parents were involved, it was through family therapy aimed at correcting presumed pathological family processes.

Theories Were Not Based on Observation

For the most part, the source of these views was theoretical rather than empirical [based on observation]. Earliest treatments evolved in the era when psychoanalysis [the branch of psychology developed by Sigmund Freud in the early twentieth century] dominated psychiatric practice. AN was seen as representing the regressed outcome of a severely dysfunctional relationship with parents around sexual desire and anxiety. Consistent with this view, patients were treated individually and encouraged to examine the destructive forces operating within their relationship with their parents. Later on, Minuchin's influential work recast the blame so as to involve the entire family's structure and interactions. His claims, like those of the psychoanalysts, have held continued appeal to therapists in spite of the fact that there is little systematic evidence to support either position.

Other approaches hold that it's developmentally appropriate to exclude parents from treatment of their adolescent son or daughter. That is, adolescents are seeking autonomy and need to separate from their families. Although this is doubtless an important process in Western culture specifically, it ignores compelling evidence that parents remain a key resource to adolescents and without them their chances of successful adulthood is diminished.

Compounding this problem, despite the obvious seriousness both medically and psychologically of AN, there are few studies to guide treatment. Only a handful of randomized clinical treatment trials of psychotherapeutic interventions for AN have been published and these are small in size and many suffer from fairly serious methodological limitations. This lack of evidence has left therapists with little guidance and has contributed to the persistent hold of theoretically driven rather than empirically driven approaches to AN.

Embracing a Parent-Positive Approach

Interestingly, what evidence we do have generally favors an approach that runs completely counter to existing theories about parents and families as the incompetent culprits that cause AN. This evidence is based on a series of family therapy studies that began in the 1980s at the Maudsley Hospital in London and have continued there and elsewhere. The approach advocated in these studies is a form of family therapy aimed at empower-

Recent studies have shown that the parents of a child with an eating disorder can positively influence the healing process.

ing families, particularly parents, to address the problems AN is causing for their child and family. Specifically, parents are disabused [freed from the belief] of the notion that they have caused AN, thus reducing guilt and the resultant fear of taking action to address it.

Further, parents learn how they can take decisive action to disrupt behaviors such as restrictive dieting, purging, and excessive exercise to forestall the eminent . . . and future severe medical and psychological problems with chronic AN. Most importantly, parents are encouraged . . . to find solutions to these problems and to persist in struggling against the powerful hold they have on their family. Data from the studies that have used this "parent positive" approach suggest that it is acceptable and effective.

A More Balanced View Is Needed

Nonetheless, parents still arrive for treatment informed through scores of books and articles, information gathered from the internet, and consultations from therapists and physicians that they somehow caused the illness and that they are helpless in the face of it. We clearly need to provide a more balanced view of how

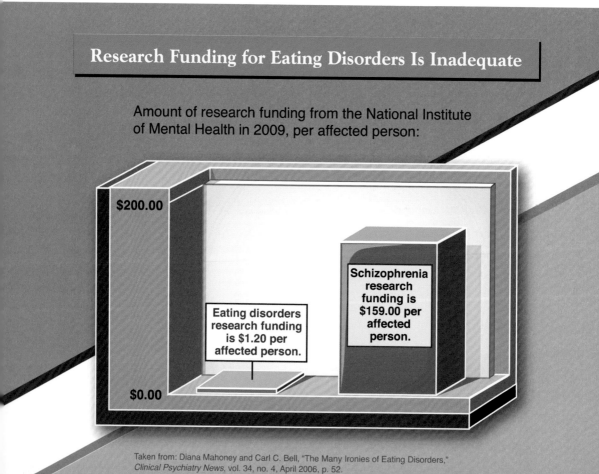

Research Funding for Eating Disorders Is Inadequate

Amount of research funding from the National Institute of Mental Health in 2009, per affected person:

$200.00

$0.00

Eating disorders research funding is $1.20 per affected person.

Schizophrenia research funding is $159.00 per affected person.

Taken from: Diana Mahoney and Carl C. Bell, "The Many Ironies of Eating Disorders," *Clinical Psychiatry News*, vol. 34, no. 4, April 2006, p. 52.

parents can be involved. In our short book [*How to Help Your Teenager Beat an Eating Disorder*], we have endeavored to employ the basic approach used by the Maudsely group to reeducate parents about AN, anchored by the following ideas:

Parents should take immediate and decisive action to forestall both the immediate medical problems associated with severe malnutrition and chronicity [long-term medical complications]. Parents must view themselves as necessary and important contributors to improvements in their child's recovery regardless of whether their child's treatment is in hospital or outpatient and whether individual or family based. And, most importantly, parents should refuse to be excluded from their child's care. In a society where anxious parenting has become the norm, we hope this book will help parents to start off seeking care with more confidence and with an understanding of the kinds of roles they can play to help their child with AN.

It is generally not reasonable to think that a parent should have expertise in how to manage AN without expert consultation and support. The illness is challenging even for those with many years of experience. However, professionals may sometimes be surprised by the ingenuity and skills parents can provide through the unique leverage that parental love and investment in their children allows.

It remains to be seen whether family therapy that sees the family as a resource to the adolescent's recovery from AN will ultimately prove to be the most efficacious approach. Studies are at last underway to determine this. But what is already quite evident is that it is not necessary to exclude families and particularly parents from treatment. Instead, it appears that they are a help rather than a hindrance.

TWELVE

Struggling with an Eating Disorder

"Jessica"

Jessica, a twenty-six-year-old from Houston, Texas, at the time she wrote this memoir, suffered for many years from a variety of eating disorders, including compulsive overeating, anorexia, and bulimia, and is now fully recovered. In the following viewpoint Jessica describes her experience with a number of eating disorders, including both anorexia and bulimia, and the many challenges she experienced in her long and difficult road to full recovery. She discusses in detail the harmful effects her eating disorder had on her family, as well as her own life, and details her experiences with various recovery programs. As is the case with many people who have eating disorders, Jessica experienced other psychological issues as well, such as cutting (self-abuse). Today she feels very lucky to have survived her eating disorder and reports feeling grateful for everything she went through, since it strengthened her character.

My life seemingly looked like I had it together. This is when I decided that I was going to lose weight, and nothing was going to get in my way! That way everything would really be perfect. That way I could really be perfect. So one of my best friends and I went on a "diet". I had tried diets countless times before and always "failed", and then was always ridiculed by my father for being fat, given suggestions by my mother on how to eat healthily. Their hearts were in the right place, my own mind was not. From there, my battle with Anorexia began. My friend quickly went off of her "diet", but I stumbled upon what—at that time—I considered being the best thing in the entire world. I could live on virtually no food, I could exercise for a really long time, and the weight fell off, and quickly. Voilà [French word expressing satisfaction], problem solved right? Wrong. Within two years I had gone from "the fat girl" to "the really sick emaciated girl". Eventually, I became weak. My hair was falling out. My teeth started getting transparent. My skin was this yellow-ish grey color. I had really dark circles under my eyes. And I had really foul breath (which is common with Anorexics). It hurt to sit down. But it hurt to stand too. I was NEVER comfortable and I was ALWAYS cold. But I never showed any of it, not even to myself. I'd always deny any of these things were real, or I'd make excuses and justifications. I started using amphetamines & marijuana, and went from being a casual smoker to smoking about a pack a day. At this point, I started cutting myself again. I felt so out of control, but I kept saying to myself "If you starve, you are IN control. If you eat you are weak and out of control". But I knew, logically I knew, I was out of control. I just wouldn't let myself (or anyone else) believe it. My parents put me in therapy, which really was pretty useless at that time, because I was in such denial, I had no desire to get better, and I lied about everything. My parents would get angry at me and frustrated with me. They'd tell me I was just trying to get attention, and that I was being selfish and self centered. Of course, I already felt worthless enough, and them saying this just made me feel worse.

Never Thin Enough

It only got worse from there. My parents divorced when I was 16 years old. My mom and I moved here to Houston.

My days and nights kind of just ran into one, it was all just one really long day—I was completely obsessed. It was almost a

At times people with eating disorders are consumed with the thought, "How little can I eat today?"

game. How little can I eat today? How much can I lose today? How long can I exercise today? One day, when I was 16 years old, I came home from school. I was walking behind a friend of mine, and she climbed up on the ledge to get to the gate to our apartment complex. I'd say the ledge was only about 4 feet tall. Well I couldn't climb up on the ledge. I was too weak, I felt as though my legs were jello, I literally just wanted to lay down on the pavement and go to sleep. I walked through the apartment door, with a fake smile plastered on my face, and my mom said "I saw you through the window; you couldn't even get up on that itty bitty ledge, Jess. . . . You're sick and you need help". I didn't know this then, but my mom told me when I was in treatment the 1st time, that she used to check on me several times in the middle of the night to make sure I was still breathing.

Of course, I thought she was out of her mind! I wasn't nearly thin enough yet, or perfect enough yet. I kept saying to myself "When I'm thin enough, then I'll start eating". Thing was, I never was thin enough. Ever. My "goal weights" kept getting lower and lower and lower. I would always ask people that I thought were skinny how much they weighed, if it was less than what I weighed, then that would be my goal weight. But when I got to that weight, I always felt and saw just as much fat, if not more, as before. So then I'd decrease my goal weight. Until it went lower and lower and lower. It was NEVER good enough, I NEVER felt good enough. I NEVER felt thin enough, or pure enough, or in control enough. But I was totally convinced that when I hit the perfect number on the scale, then I finally would feel on top of the world.

I will never forget that one day a group of girls came up to me at school and asked me if I had Cancer, to this day, 10 years later, I remember what I was wearing on that particular day. I was wearing my favorite outfit—the one that made me look the thinnest! Ironically enough the same night my mom said to me while we were in the grocery store, with a really disturbed look on her face that I looked like I was dying of cancer. . . .

Purging for the First Time

I remember the very first time I purged. One of the very few things I would eat was this one particular Chinese restaurant, on the other side of town. So my mom would make the drive and we'd go eat together, God my poor mother. The things I put that woman through (throwing plates of food at her head, for one, screaming at her, causing such worry, etc.) On one particular day, I decided I wanted to go eat (which was like a hallmark-moment in our house), so my mom took me to the Chinese restaurant. Normally, I just pushed the food around on my plate, nibbled here and there, but never really consumed all that much. But this day was different. I finished several full plates of food. I am sure my mom was shocked! I hadn't finished an entire meal in years. Of course I became panic stricken, so I went into the bathroom with the intent of purging, but the bathroom was really crowded, and

I just couldn't bring myself to do it around other people. I knew what I had to do, even if I had to wait until I got home to do it, the food WAS coming out of me.

And so the drive home was excruciating. The anxiety, the fear, the panic, the silent tears. . . . I about wanted to crawl out of my skin.

What is normally a 25 minute car ride, seemed like days.

Finally we got home.

And I purged for the first time.

That's when the bargaining began "OK, I will only do this in desperate situations. . . . Only when absolutely necessary".

But over a short period of time, the frequency of my binge/purge episodes drastically increased, going from maybe once every two weeks, to several times a day. Anorexia was now a memory, and Bulimia was my life. . . .

Things Got Worse in College

I changed therapists at this point, to an eating disorders specialist, because I had no good luck with any of my previous therapists. I don't know if that was because of my lack of willingness, or their ignorance.

In 1998 I went off to college. . . . I stopped bingeing and purging, and started starving myself again. Not only was I swimming several hours a day, but I was at the gym all of the time. At school I had free reign to do whatever my little heart desired and no one could stop me! So I ran with the "opportunity". I started using amphetamines again. And drinking quite a bit. I had dropped some weight, the cutting was out of control, and I began exhibiting symptoms of mental illness. Just short of the 1st semester, I had a nervous breakdown, called my mom to come pick me up, and left college.

I moved in with my new boyfriend, and the eating disorder, self injury, and mental illness symptoms continued. At this point I had upped the stakes to daily laxative, diet pill, and diuretic abuse.

Within a year I wound up in the E.R. with rectal hemorrhaging.

Therapy Was Difficult but Helpful

I started going to Texas Children's Hospital to see a doctor that specialized in eating disorders. Man, I hated that woman!! She saw RIGHT through me, she called me on ALL my lies, she was really strict, and told me how it was. While part of me wanted to hate her, I also knew she could really help me, and for that I respected her. And I really did want help. I got put on a Halter Monitor (it's like a portable EKG machine that you have to wear strapped to you, and then you return it to the doctors, and the doctors review the results to see what your heart patterns are like—normal or abnormal). Six months passed, before my treatment team determined I had to go inpatient. I was 20 years old.

I spent 7 weeks at a treatment center in Florida, and had a very positive experience there. The staff was wonderful, the women I was there with and I became very close. But it was A LOT of hard work, very tiring, and so hard facing all the things that I had run from since childhood. I had been on psychiatric meds for a while at this point, but they changed all my meds while I was there, and did a complete psychiatric work up on me.

A Series of Relapses

I left the treatment center shortly before Halloween of 2000.

And this is where my "affair" with relapse begins.

For the first year after I got out of treatment, I did extremely well. I had my "slips" behavior wise, but was more so on the up and up. My thought patterns though, had quickly reverted back to the way I had thought before I went to treatment. The worthlessness, the anxiety, the fear, the need for perfection, wanting to numb out, etc. I don't remember how or when I relapsed for the first time. When I say relapse, I want to make it clear that there is a difference between a "relapse" and a "lapse". A relapse is when you stay stuck in eating disorder behavior, when you are so obsessed you lose touch with reality. A "lapse" is a normal part of recovery, you fall—you get up—you brush yourself off—you try again.

[During] the years 2002–2005 I went to another residential treatment facility for a week long eating disorder intensive program, did an IOP [intensive outpatient program] program for five and a half months, and was in the psychiatric hospital for my eating disorder and self injury on 3 different occasions. Not to mention in therapy, therapy, therapy, I had begun seeing a dietician once a week, and started seeing a new psychiatrist once a month. During this time period I had been on just about every psychiatric medication out there, on heavy doses of them, and at one point I was up to 7 different kinds every day! I became addicted to one of my medications, abusing it as a way to not feel. It made me numb. At this point I was in such pain, I needed to be numb. One evening, I intentionally overdosed. I was fed up, done, through. I couldn't live the way I was living anymore. I was in too much pain, and I was causing too much pain. Within about three to five minutes after taking the pills, I came to my senses [about] what I had just done, realized I really did not want to die, freaked out, and purged up all the pills.

Lucky to Be Alive

I had already somehow miraculously defeated death on more than one occasion. I remember going to bed every night (when I'd actually allow myself sleep) and I prayed and prayed and prayed to a higher-being (if there was one) to please please spare my life, if my life was spared, I would never act out on my eating disorder again. And my life was spared, for years and years; I woke up every day, only to start the cycle all over again. I also had programmed 9-1-1 into my portable phone, and every time I went to purge, I would take the phone with me into the bathroom and have it set to dial just in case something happened and I had a heart attack, or purged too much blood, or something else catastrophic. . . .

I got out of the hospital the day before Thanksgiving 2005. . . .

My therapist whom I had been seeing since 1998 had told me that she was no longer going to be seeing clients on an individual basis, and she was just going to be running the IOP program (and I was not in the program at that time), so she would not be able

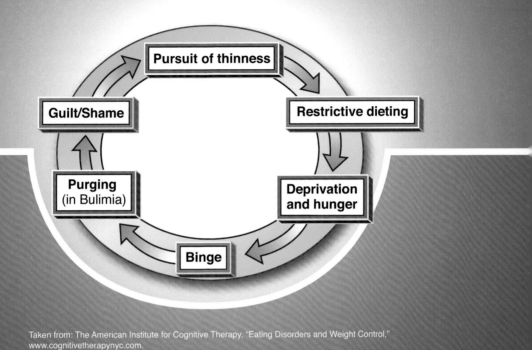

The Vicious Cycle of Eating Disorders

- Pursuit of thinness
- Restrictive dieting
- Deprivation and hunger
- Binge
- Purging (in Bulimia)
- Guilt/Shame

Taken from: The American Institute for Cognitive Therapy, "Eating Disorders and Weight Control," www.cognitivetherapynyc.com.

to see me anymore. She also said that even if that wasn't the case, she would most likely [have] referred me to somebody else. I was so upset! I had been seeing her since 1998!! I looked up to her and admired her. I felt like a really big failure at this point, because she said she would have referred me out, in my mind meaning that I was a) untreatable b) I let her down. This was one of the most admirable women I had ever met. She never gave up hope that I would recover. She believed in me, when very very few people did. I truly believe had it not been for her, I would have given up. Stopping therapy with her was one of the hardest things I have had to do in my life. She will forever hold a special place in my heart. It is now, in hindsight, that I see that everything really does happen for a reason, and while we may not like it—or agree with it—at the time, eventually we see the meaning behind everything.

A Dramatic Improvement

I started seeing a new therapist, an eating disorders specialist who I had a history with because I went to her support group on and off for several years, so I already felt comfortable with her, and she knew some of my history. One of my best friends also sees this therapist, and she has a lot of experience and good results. So there was no doubt in my mind that I wanted to start seeing her. I continued seeing my dietician and psychiatrist as well.

I started seeing a great deal of improvement almost immediately. My thinking began to change, I became able to cry again, the only time I had really ever cried in years was when I was at the hospital. My eating disorder behaviors drastically decreased, the cutting stopped completely. I began seeing the world "in color" rather than in "black and white". The glass went from half empty to half full. I don't know, it's weird. It's almost like one day I just had this "awakening", and I knew everything was going to be just fine. I knew I was going to be OK. It happened, just like that. . . . I don't know why it happened when it did, and at this point I don't much care. I am just grateful it did. I try not to analyze or judge but just accept and use the knowledge I have gained towards a positive attitude and healthy and balanced lifestyle.

The Journey to Full Recovery

Recovery from my eating disorder, strong solid recovery, was made up of a lot of ups and downs. A lot of feelings and emotions, sometimes I felt like I was just going to explode. I still lived in a lot of fear and doubt. Doubt that I could ever fully recover; fear that I would fail once again. I was TERRIFIED about stepping into the unknown, into unfamiliar territory. But what it came down to for me was this: The risk it would be to get into and stick with recovery was FAR LESS than the risk I would be taking staying sick, risking my sanity, and eventually the inevitable: death. I had already had 2 friends of mine die from their eating disorders (and one was at a "normal" weight!! You can DIE from an eating disorder at ANY weight!! Eating disorders are NOT about the number on the scale).

Today, life is good. I am HAPPY (yes, I still have my bad days though!), I have peace and serenity today. I have an identity today. I have a social life. I know how to genuinely smile and laugh and FEEL. I don't have that blank lifeless look in my eyes, my eyes glow. . . . I eat "normally", I never think about the eating disorder or self injury—and if ever I do think about it it's more like I think about the fact that I don't think about it! I am down to just an anti-depressant every day, and then an anti-psychotic PRN (as needed).

Today I consider myself recovered. It's such a wild feeling. It feels like a huge accomplishment, it has totally put a different perspective on the way I perceive and process things. While I often wonder what my life would have been like had I not developed an eating disorder or become a cutter, and while I wish more than anything that I could have spared myself and my parents the pain we all went through during my many years being sick, I have to say I have no regrets. Going through what I have been through, has shaped who I am as a person today. I truly believe I am a more authentic, more genuine, more accepting, and more insightful person because of my struggles and latter journey through recovery.

What You Should Know About Eating Disorders

Facts About Eating Disorders

- Between 0.5 percent and 3.7 percent of females suffer from anorexia nervosa in their lifetime.
- Anorexia is the third most common chronic illness among adolescents.
- Between 1.1 percent and 4.2 percent of females suffer from bulimia nervosa in their lifetime.
- Between 2 percent and 5 percent of the American population experience binge-eating disorder.
- Eating disorders affect up to 24 million Americans and 70 million individuals worldwide.
- In 1994 *Essence* magazine reported that 53.5 percent of African American females who responded to their survey were at risk of an eating disorder.
- At least 10 percent to 15 percent of people with anorexia or bulimia are male; one Harvard study found that men make up a quarter of anorexia and bulimia cases and close to 40 percent of binge eaters.
- A Cornell University study found that 40 percent of male football players surveyed engaged in some sort of disordered eating behavior.
- Forty percent of newly identified cases of anorexia are in girls from fifteen to nineteen years old; since 1930 each decade has seen an increase in anorexia among girls in that age group.

- The incidence of bulimia in females aged ten to thirty-nine tripled between 1988 and 1993.
- Fifteen percent of young women in the United States who are not diagnosed with an eating disorder display substantially disordered eating attitudes and behaviors.
- More than half of teenage girls and almost a third of teenage boys use unhealthy weight control behaviors such as skipping meals, fasting, smoking cigarettes, vomiting, and taking laxatives.
- Eating disorders can coexist, or people can switch from one eating disorder to another; for example, from anorexia to bulimia.
- Low self-esteem is the most common characteristic of those suffering from eating disorders.

Dieting and Eating Disorders

- Girls who frequently diet are twelve times as likely to binge as girls who do not diet.
- Eighty-one percent of ten-year-olds are afraid of being fat. Fifty-one percent of nine- and ten-year-old girls feel better about themselves when they are on a diet.
- Eighty percent of children have been on a diet by the time they have reached the fourth grade.
- Forty-six percent of nine- to eleven-year-olds are "sometimes" or "very often" on diets, and 82 percent of their families are "sometimes" or "very often" on diets.
- Ninety-one percent of women recently surveyed on a college campus had attempted to control their weight through dieting; 22 percent dieted "often" or "always."
- Twenty-five percent of American men and 45 percent of American women are on a diet on any given day.
- Thirty-five percent of "normal dieters" progress to pathological dieting. Of those, 20 percent to 25 percent progress to partial or full-syndrome eating disorders.
- The diet-related industry is a 50-billion-dollar-a-year enterprise.

Eating Disorder Behaviors and Effects

- Physical effects of eating disorders include malnutrition and dehydration; heart, kidney, and liver damage; ruptured stomach and tears to the esophagus; changes in brain structure; and many other harmful short- and long-term effects.
- Psychological impacts of eating disorders include depression, low self-esteem, shame and guilt, mood swings, and anxiety.
- Eating disorder risk may be increased by a history of psychiatric problems such as substance abuse, depression, or anxiety. Sexual, physical and/or emotional abuse is very common in those suffering from eating disorders, although not all those suffering from eating disorders have experienced such abuse.
- Behaviors frequently associated with eating disorders include starvation, restriction of food, bingeing, and purging.
- Many anorexics or bulimics are addicted to junk food, which can satisfy cravings or give quick energy with little or no nutritional value.
- An eating disorder sufferer may replace food with drugs, including alcohol, coffee, and cigarettes, among others.
- In the early stages of recovery, some people may substitute excessive exercise for restricting or purging behaviors; excessive exercise taken to extremes can also be unhealthy and dangerous.

Treatment of Eating Disorders

- Early and appropriate treatment can greatly improve the outcome for someone with an eating disorder.
- Only one-third of people with anorexia receive mental health care; only 6 percent of people with bulimia receive mental health care.
- Three-quarters of Americans believe eating disorders should be covered by insurance companies like any other illness, yet health insurance companies often cover little or none of the cost of treatment.
- Eating disorder treatment can be very expensive; inpatient treatment can be $30,000 or more per month, while outpatient treatment can end up costing over $100,000.

- Despite the high prevalence of eating disorders in America, few states have adequate programs to treat them, and few schools and colleges have programs educating youth about the dangers of these illnesses.
- Five percent to 10 percent of anorexics die within ten years of onset, and 18 percent to 20 percent die within twenty years of onset. Young women with anorexia are twelve times more likely to die than women the same age without anorexia. Causes of death include suicide and heart problems.
- Eighty-six percent of people with eating disorders report onset by age twenty (10 percent report onset at age ten or younger; 33 percent report onset between ages eleven and fifteen, and 43 percent between ages sixteen and twenty).
- Thirty percent of patients report their eating disorder lasted from one to five years; 31 percent from six to ten years, and 16 percent report duration from eleven to fifteen years.
- Almost half of anorexia patients recover, and an additional 33 percent improve to some degree.
- About half of bulimic individuals recover, and an additional 30 percent improve to some degree. Ten years after the onset of the illness, only 10 percent of bulimics meet the diagnostic criteria for bulimia.
- Successful treatment of eating disorders often involves a team consisting of treatment providers from different health disciplines, such as psychologists, psychotherapists, physicians, dietitians, and nurses.

What You Should Do About Eating Disorders

Gather Information

The first step in grappling with any complex and controversial issue is to be informed about it. Gather as much information as you can from a variety of sources. The essays in this book form an excellent starting point, representing a variety of viewpoints and approaches to the topic. Your school or local library will be another source of useful information; look there for relevant books, magazines, and encyclopedia entries. The bibliography and "Organizations to Contact" sections of this book will give you useful starting points in gathering additional information.

The last couple of decades have seen an enormous increase in the amount of information available on eating disorders. There are many scientific articles available on all aspects of disordered eating which may be helpful to you. If the information in such articles is too dense or technical, check the abstract at the beginning of the article, which provides a clear summary of the researcher's conclusions.

Internet search engines will be helpful to you in your search. You may also want to find and interview people who have suffered from or treat eating disorders. In many areas there are support groups you can talk to, or you may be able to contact such groups by phone or the Internet (start with the "Organizations to Contact" section of this book).

Identify the Issues Involved

Once you have gathered your information, review it methodically to discover the key issues involved. What theories do people have about the cause(s) of eating disorders? How effective are the treatments for eating disorders? How prevalent are eating disorders, and who is most affected by them? Have ideas about eating disorders changed over time? It is worthwhile to consider how eating disorders have manifested in other cultures and time periods, which provides a broader perspective on what is happening in America today.

You may find that the type of treatment approach favored depends largely on what is believed to be the primary cause of the eating disorder. Some people may consider the cause to be primarily physical in origin—for example, an imbalance in brain chemistry or hormones—and will consequently favor medicines that seek to restore normal functioning. Others will focus on psychological or emotional issues and favor psychotherapy or counseling or blame cultural influences and promote changes in the media. You may also discover that different approaches are believed to work better for different eating disorders—for example, a treatment approach that may work for many anorexics may be less successful in treating bulimia.

Evaluate Your Information Sources

In developing your own opinion, it is vital to evaluate the sources of the information you have discovered. Authors of books, magazine articles, and so forth, however well intentioned, have their own perspective and biases that may affect how they present information on the subject. Much remains unknown about eating disorders, and new information and research is coming to light all the time. Even experts on eating disorders often have very different ideas about what causes the various disorders and how best to treat them.

Consider the authors' credentials and what organizations they are affiliated with. For example, an article by a social activist working for a media watchdog organization will probably focus on media portrayals of beauty. On the other hand, an article from the *Journal of Clinical Psychiatry* would more likely emphasize chemical imbalances and treatments that attempt to correct them. Both articles may offer information that is perfectly valid, but each will present data that support the author's viewpoint and that of the organizations they are associated with. Critically evaluate and assess your sources rather than take whatever they say at face value.

Examine Your Own Perspective

Eating disorders are an emotionally charged issue involving body image, self-esteem, and cultural and family influences. Spend some time exploring your own thoughts and feelings about the various pieces of the eating disorders puzzle and how they fit together in your own life. The messages you have received from family members, friends, and the media throughout your life will affect your own thoughts and feelings. How do you feel about your body? Do you have a healthy relationship with food and exercise? How do your friends and family members relate to food and body issues? Have you or people you know engaged in any of the disordered eating patterns you have learned about?

Perhaps you or someone you love has suffered, or is suffering, from an eating disorder or is showing some of the behaviors or characteristics associated with disordered eating; if so, this may make it more challenging to form a clear view of the issues involved in eating disorders.

Form an Opinion and Take Action

Once you have gathered and organized information, identified the issues involved, and examined your own perspective, you will be ready to form an opinion on eating disorders and to advocate your position in debates and discussions. (And if you or someone you love has problems with disordered eating, you will have a better idea of how to begin the needed journey of healing and self-discovery.) Perhaps you will conclude that one of the approaches you have encountered is the most important factor in explaining and treating eating disorders, or you may decide that a variety of factors working together determine whether and how eating disorders show up in people. You might even decide that none of the perspectives on eating disorders is entirely convincing to you and that you cannot take a decisive position as yet. If that is the case, ask yourself what you would need to know to make up your mind; perhaps a bit more research would be helpful. Whatever position you take, be prepared to explain it clearly based on facts, evidence, and well-thought-out beliefs.

ORGANIZATIONS TO CONTACT

The editors have compiled the following list of organizations concerned with the issues debated in this book. The descriptions are derived from materials provided by the organizations. All have publications or information available for interested readers. The list was compiled on the date of publication of the present volume; the information provided here may change. Be aware that many organizations take several weeks or longer to respond to inquiries, so allow as much time as possible for the receipt of requested materials.

Academy for Eating Disorders (AED)
111 Deer Lake Rd., Ste. 100, Deerfield, IL 60015
(847) 498-4274
e-mail: info@aedweb.org
Web site: www.aedweb.org

The AED is a global professional association devoted to eating disorders research, education, treatment, and prevention. It promotes the effective treatment and care of patients with eating disorders and associated disorders, supports research in the field, and disseminates knowledge regarding eating disorders.

Alliance for Eating Disorders Awareness
PO Box 13155, North Palm Beach, FL 33408-3155
(561) 841-0900
e-mail: info@eatingdisorderinfo.org
Web site: www.eatingdisorderinfo.org

The Alliance for Eating Disorders Awareness is a nonprofit organization working to prevent eating disorders and promote a positive body image, free from weight preoccupation and size prejudice. The alliance offers educational presentations, information and referral, training, advocacy, support, and mentoring services.

Binge Eating Disorder Association (BEDA)
550M Ritchie Hwy., Ste. 271, Severna Park, MD 21146
(443) 597-0066
e-mail: info@bedaonline.com
Web site: www.bedaonline.com

BEDA was founded to help those who have binge-eating disorder, their friends and family, and those who treat the disorder. BEDA provides the individuals who suffer from binge-eating disorder with recognition and resources to begin a safe journey toward a healthy recovery. The association also serves as a resource for providers of all kinds to prevent, diagnose, and treat the disorder.

Eating Disorders Anonymous (EDA)
General Service Board of EDA, Inc.
PO Box 55876, Phoenix, AZ 85078-5876
e-mail: info@eatingdisordersanonymous.org
Web site: www.eatingdisordersanonymous.org

EDA is a fellowship of individuals who share their experience, strength, and hope with each other so that they may solve their common problems and help others to recover from their eating disorders. EDA endorses sound nutrition and discourages any form of rigidity around food. Its Web site offers written materials on eating disorders, and volunteers host online, in-person, and phone meetings.

Eating Disorders Coalition (EDC)
720 Seventh St. NW, Ste. 300, Washington, DC 20001
(202) 543-9570
e-mail: manager@eatingdisorderscoalition.org
Web site: www.eatingdisorderscoalition.org

The EDC aims to advance the federal recognition of eating disorders as a public health priority, to raise awareness among policy makers and the public at large about the serious health risk posed by eating disorders, and to mobilize concerned citizens to advocate on behalf of people with eating disorders, their families, and professionals working with these populations. The coalition promotes legislation that will help to achieve these goals.

Jessie's Wish
742 Colony Forest Dr., Midlothian, VA 23114
(804) 378-3032
e-mail: jessieswish@verizon.net
Web site: www.jessieswish.org

Jessie's Wish is a nonprofit organization that seeks to help individuals suffering from eating disorders, and their families, by providing education on the devastating effects of eating disorders and by helping with financial assistance when health insurance is inadequate or not available.

The Joy Project
PO Box 16488, St. Paul, MN 55116
e-mail: volunteercoordinator@joyproject.org
Web site: www.joyproject.org

The Joy Project is a nonprofit, grassroots organization based on the philosophy of using real-world, workable solutions to end the epidemic of eating disorders. It works toward reducing the rate and severity of eating disorders by supporting and conducting research, education, and support programs.

Multi-service Eating Disorders Association (MEDA)
92 Pearl St., Newton, MA 02458
(617) 558-1881
e-mail: info@medainc.org
Web site: www.medainc.org

MEDA is a nonprofit organization dedicated to the prevention and treatment of eating disorders and disordered eating. The association's mission is to prevent the continuing spread of eating disorders through educational awareness and early detection. MEDA serves as a support network and resource for clients, loved ones, clinicians, educators, and the general public.

National Association of Anorexia and Associated Disorders (ANAD)
PO Box 640, Naperville, IL 60566
(630) 577-1333 • Helpline: (630) 577-1330
e-mail: anadhelp@anad.org
Web site: www.anad.org

ANAD is a nonprofit corporation that seeks to prevent and alleviate the problems of eating disorders, especially including anorexia nervosa, bulimia nervosa, and binge-eating disorder. Over 200 ANAD support groups provide support and self-help for the individuals and families affected by eating disorders, free of charge.

National Center for Overcoming Overeating
350 W. 50th St., Ste. 34E, New York, NY 10019
(212) 582-0383
e-mail: webmaster@overcomingovereating.com
Web site: www.overcomingovereating.com

The National Center for Overcoming Overeating is an educational and training organization working to end body hatred and dieting. It was started in 1989 by Carol Munter and Jane Hirschmann, authors of *Overcoming Overeating* and *When Women Stop Hating Their Bodies*; Hirshmann also coauthored *Preventing Childhood Eating Problems*. Video and written materials are available to help overcome overeating without dieting.

The National Eating Disorder Information Center (NEDIC)
ES 7-421, 200 Elizabeth St., Toronto, ON M5G 2C4
(416) 340-4156
e-mail: nedic@uhn.on.ca
Web site: www.nedic.ca

The NEDIC is a nonprofit organization founded in 1985 to provide information and resources on eating disorders and food and weight preoccupation, and to inform the public about eating disorders and related issues.

National Eating Disorders Association (NEDA)
603 Stewart St., Ste. 803, Seattle, WA 98101
(206) 382-3587 • Helpline: (800) 931-2237
e-mail: info@NationalEatingDisorders.org
Web site: www.nationaleatingdisorders.org

NEDA supports individuals and families affected by eating disorders and serves as a catalyst for prevention, cures, and access to quality care. It campaigns for prevention, improved access to quality treatment, and increased research funding to better understand and treat eating disorders. In 1999 NEDA established a toll-free helpline and has helped more than fifty thousand people find appropriate treatment.

National Eating Disorders Screening Program (NEDSP)
One Washington St., Ste. 304, Wellesley Hills, MA 02481
(781) 239-0071
e-mail: smhinfo@mentalhealthscreening.org
Web site: www.mentalhealthscreening.org/events/nedsp/index
.aspx

The NEDSP focuses on the three main types of eating disorders—anorexia nervosa, bulimia nervosa, and binge-eating disorder. The goal of the program is to raise the level of awareness about eating disorders and to encourage people who may be suffering from eating disorders to seek further help and treatment.

The Renfrew Center Foundation
475 Spring Ln., Philadelphia, PA 19128
(877) 367-3383
e-mail: foundation@renfrew.org
Web site: www.renfrew.org

The Renfrew Center, founded in 1985, is America's first free-standing facility exclusively dedicated to the treatment of eating disorders. It provides public and professional education to increase awareness of anorexia, bulimia, and binge-eating disorder though educational programs, communication with policy makers, and research.

BIBLIOGRAPHY

Books

Stephanie Covington Armstrong, *Not All Black Girls Know How to Eat: A Story of Bulimia*. Chicago: Lawrence Hill, 2009.

Sue Cooper and Peggy Norton, *Conquering Eating Disorders: How Family Communication Heals*. Berkeley, CA: Seal, 2008.

Carolyn Costin, *100 Questions & Answers About Anorexia Nervosa*. Sudbury, MA: Jones and Bartlett, 2007.

Sheryle Cruse, *Thin Enough: My Spiritual Journey Through the Living Death of an Eating Disorder*. Birmingham, AL: New Hope, 2006.

Eve Ensler, *The Good Body*. New York: Villard, 2004.

Lesli J. Favor, *Food as Foe: Nutrition and Eating Disorders*. Tarrytown, NY: Marshall Cavendish, 2007.

Gary A. Grahl, *Skinny Boy: A Young Man's Battle and Triumph over Anorexia*. Clearfield, UT: American Legacy Media, 2007.

Mark J. Kittleson and Gerri Freid Kramer, eds., *The Truth About Eating Disorders*. New York: Facts On File, 2004.

Jenny Langley, *Boys Get Anorexia Too: Coping with Male Eating Disorders in the Family*. London: Sage, 2006.

Sandra Augustyn Lawton, ed., *Eating Disorders Information for Teens: Health Tips About Anorexia, Bulimia, Binge Eating, and Other Eating Disorders*. 2nd ed. Detroit: Omnigraphics, 2009.

Katie Metcalfe, *Anorexia: A Stranger in the Family*. Bedlinog, Mid-Glamorgan, Wales: Accent, 2006.

Anna Patterson, *Fit to Die: Men and Eating Disorders*. London: Sage, 2004.

Jennifer Sey, *Chalked Up: Inside Elite Gymnastics' Merciless Coaching, Overzealous Parents, Eating Disorders, and Elusive Olympic Dreams*. New York: HarperCollins, 2008.

Kate Taylor, ed., *Going Hungry: Writers on Desire, Self-Denial, and Overcoming Anorexia*. New York: Random House, 2008.

Periodicals

Darla Atlas, "The Thin Line: Moms, Daughters and Eating," *Dallas Morning News*, October 31, 2006.

Denise Brodey, "Blacks Join the Eating-Disorder Mainstream," *New York Times*, September 20, 2005.

Jennifer Chancellor, "Waisting Away: Signs for Detecting Eating Disorders in Preteen Girls," *Tulsa World*, March 4, 2007.

Margena A. Christian, "What Black Women Need to Know About Eating Disorders," *Jet*, September 25, 2006.

Kristine Crane, "Compelled to Be Thin: Women in Their 30s Confront Eating Disorders," *Charlotte (NC) Observer*, August 21, 2008.

Hilary de Vries, "Why We're at War with Our Bodies," *Marie Claire*, July 2006.

Abby Ellin, "What's Eating Our Kids? Fears About 'Bad' Foods," *New York Times*, February 26, 2009.

Kristen Kemp, "Special Report: Weighing In," *Girls' Life*, June/July 2006.

Donna Koehn, "Barbie Isn't the Only One with an Impossible Physique," *Tampa (FL) Tribune*, September 30, 2007.

Joan Lippert, Jill Shea, and Martha Seagrave, "Anorexia Nervosa: Dying to Be Thin," *Clinical Advisor*, April 2008.

Amelia McDonell-Parry, "Wanna Rexia," *Teen Vogue*, February 2008.

Melba Newsome, "Not Just for Kids: Why Anorexia and Bulimia Are on the Rise in Women Confronting Their Midlife Years," *Time*, September 5, 2005.

Elizabeth Palmberg, "Body Language," *Sojourners*, April 2009.

Hibi Pendleton, "Off the Deep End; as Teenage Athletes, Two Sisters Grappled with the Pressure to Stay Thin," *Vogue*, January 2008.

Lesley Rotchford, "Why Women's Eating Habits Get So out of Whack," *Cosmopolitan*, September 2007.

Geneen Roth, "Why Am I Eating This?" *Prevention*, May 2006.

Shelly Sinton, "Healthy Eating May Be Hazardous to Your Health," *She Knows Diet & Fitness*, February/March 2006.

Sheba R. Wheeler, "Secret Sickness Hidden Obsession," *Denver Post*, May 5, 2008.

Emily Yoffe, "Stuffed!" O: *The Oprah Magazine*, August 2007.

PICTURE CREDITS